한마음 장로교회
One Mind Presbyterian Church

EDUCATOR'S LIFETIME LIBRARY

of

Stories, Quotes, Anecdotes, Wit and Humor

Also by the Authors:

Personalized Behavioral Modification: Practical Techniques for Elementary Educators

Handbook of Discovery Techniques in Elementary School Teaching

EDUCATOR'S LIFETIME LIBRARY

of

Stories, Quotes, Anecdotes, Wit and Humor

P. Susan Mamchak

and

Steven R. Mamchak

PARKER PUBLISHING COMPANY, INC.
West Nyack, N.Y.

© 1979 *by*

PARKER PUBLISHING COMPANY, INC.

West Nyack, N.Y.

20   19   18   17   16   15   14   13

Library of Congress Cataloging in Publication Data

Mamchak, P   Susan
    Educator's lifetime library of stories, quotes,
anecdotes, wit, and humor.

    Includes index.
    1. Education--Anecdotes, facetiae, satire, etc.
2. Educators--Anecdotes, facetiae, satire, etc.
I. Mamchak, Steven R., joint author. II. Title.
LA23.M34   370'.2'07   78-25748
ISBN 0-13-240705-1

Printed in the United States of America

DEDICATION

. . . to Mildred M. Mamchak

and

the memory of Carrie C. Pease . . .

HOW THIS BOOK WILL
BE HELPFUL TO
PROFESSIONAL EDUCATORS

The professional educator is in a unique position. In no other profession is a person called upon to speak before groups of people *every day*. A doctor speaks with *individual* patients; a lawyer addresses a jury *occasionally;* and the clergy, when they speak, have their text dictated by the Ultimate Speaker. An educator, on the other hand, speaks before groups, speaks day in and day out to a diverse audience, and is responsible for his own material.

Not only must the educator effectively address classes each day, but, as a professional, he or she is constantly being called upon to speak before fellow faculty members, parents' organizations, community groups, and Boards of Education, as well as being asked to act as speaker, host, moderator, or M.C. at retirement dinners, conventions, luncheons, in-service training sessions, and so on. Quite often, the approach must be as diversified as the audience.

While this is evident to every experienced educator, the problem has always been threefold:

1. How to give an effective, stimulating and memorable speech or classroom presentation . . .

2. Where to find witty, humorous, dignified and appropriate material . . .

7

3. How to efficiently and intelligently overcome any problems that may arise . . .

It was these problems, among others, which occasioned the writing of this book. Until now, the educator has gone from source to source to find solutions. Now, however, there is a single source, a "Library," if you will, to which educators may go to find the type of materials which they may use on countless occasions and in numberless situations, materials which are eminently practical, totally useable, and tailored to the specialized needs of the professional educator. This book is large and encyclopedic in nature not out of design but out of *necessity,* for the wide range and scope of materials included makes this the most complete volume of its kind, one you may use now and for a lifetime to follow.

When giving an effective, stimulating and memorable speech or presentation, we have found a proven, dependable formula for success. We call it the P*R*E*P*A*R*E formula. Each letter stands for one block in the foundation of a good speech:

"P"–Preparing and Pinpointing Your Topic

For example, if you are asked to speak on "Education," your first question would be, "What phase of Education?" To give a loose, rambling speech only makes an audience restless. Therefore, make every effort to limit your topic and pinpoint a specific area which you can cover in depth within your allotted speaking time.

When asked to speak, you should ask certain questions:

What is the make-up of your audience?
How many people will you be addressing?
Where will your speech fit into the total program for that evening/afternoon?
What event, activity, speech, etc. is to proceed/follow you?
What speaking facilities (Microphone? Podium? Dais? Head Table/Audience? Stage/Audience?) are available?
How much will your audience know (or think they know) about your topic before you speak?

How does the program coordinator conceive of your speech? (Entertainment? Informative? Persuasive?)
What is the maximum and the minimum time you are to speak?

In short, you should ask any question which you feel might have a bearing on the physical environment and/or content of your speech. This attention to detail will help you prepare the right speech for the right audience at the right time. Would you, for example, give a forty-five minute speech if you were speaking just *before* dinner was to be served? Or, would you give a serious speech at a parent-child banquet where Santa Claus' appearance was to follow yours? Pinpointing your topic and preparing for the physical surroundings of your speech is your first step on the road to success.

"R"–Researching for Success

Obviously, you need to know what you are talking about. Few speakers deliberately try to mislead or misinform the audience, but trusting to memory is risky at best and disastrous at worst. It is at this point that you begin to prepare yourself to meet your audience. Consequently, you will need some information:

What will your audience want to know?
What kinds of questions will they ask?
What kinds of humor would they find best?
What would antagonize them?
What would please them?

Once you have determined the answers to these questions, you can begin your research.

Compile the information you need. If you are going to speak about a person, find out about him; if it's a current issue, review the local newspapers; use Part I of this book to select appropriate anecdotes, stories, and humor. Remember that the *quality* of your research will pave the way for a successful speech.

"E"–Examples and Their Use

Throughout a speech, good speakers use examples to prove or clarify their points. To get the most out of the examples you use, you might find these hints helpful:

1. The example should be appropriate. It must make the point you want it to make. To use an anecdote, however clever or delightful, that has no bearing on what you are saying will only confuse your audience.

2. The example should be understood by everyone. To describe two fellow educators as, "The Castor and Pollux of the educational world," is fine—providing your audience knows who Castor and Pollux were! Otherwise, the analogy is lost.

3. Avoid "inside" jokes. Every profession has its "inside" humor—those anecdotes and stories that are only amusing to those persons in that particular profession. To use such material before a "mixed" audience could lead to confusion and antagonism. Therefore, they are better left untold.

"P"–Presentation and Poise

Once you have written your speech you will, eventually, have to give it before an audience. Therefore, this phase of preparation is vital. Whether this is your first speech or your hundred and first, you should rehearse it thoroughly before you set foot in front of an audience. Sequester yourself, if need be, and stand in front of a mirror. See yourself as others will see you. Pay attention to your gestures; your eye contact; how you use your notes; your posture. Record your speech and listen to it with an open mind. Are you speaking too slowly? Too fast? In a monotone? Are your words distinct? Finally, decide what you will wear that day. Since you already know what type of function you are attending, you won't be wearing a leisure outfit to a black-tie dinner, but make an effort to select clothes in which you look best and feel best. If you feel good about your appearance, you will project confidence to your audience.

"A"–Analyzing Your Audience

When you have arrived at the place where you are to speak, you will have the opportunity to analyze your audience. Look at them, listen to them, and particularly pay attention to their reactions. Is the atmosphere formal or informal? Are they quiet and respectful or noisy and restless? If there are other speakers before you, how were they received? Your analysis of the audience will tell you what approach to take when it becomes your time to speak. Even a prepared speech may be delivered in several ways. It can be formal, conversational, or even intimate, as friend to friend. Your approach will be determined by your perception of the audience.

Finally, once you begin speaking, you will *feel* your audience. There is no way to describe this; it must be experienced. Through this rapport, this psychological bond, if you will, the audience will tell you what they think of your speech. You must take your cues from them and adjust accordingly.

"R"–Relaxing and Enjoying Yourself

In most cases, your audience *wants* you to succeed. They are on your side. If you have done all in your power to make your speech entertaining, informative, clear and concise, then you need only do one more thing to insure your speech's success—relax and enjoy yourself. If you are nervous, your audience will be nervous. If you are uncomfortable, your audience will be uncomfortable. But if you are enjoying yourself—*so will your audience.*

Speaking before people can be a truly enjoyable experience. If you really believe that and learn to enjoy speaking, then you will be a good speaker. If you don't believe it, if it is nothing more than a task, and an arduous one at that, then don't worry about it—you won't be asked to do it often. Be at ease, enjoy your audience, and you will be in demand.

"E"–Enthusiasm and Empathy: Keys to Success

Be enthusiastic—believe in what you are saying. If you are, then even if your audience does not agree with what you are saying, they will still respect you as a person of knowledge and conviction. Your enthusiasm can build a lasting positive impression in the minds of your audience. And if your speech will be followed by a question and answer period, you will find that enthusiasm is your greatest ally.

When dealing with those questions from your audience, *Empathy* is the keynote. Put yourself in the position of the questioner. If you do this, you will never slough off a question or make light of it, or the person who asked it. There will be no need to become defensive, and, because you have done your research, you can answer the question straight-forwardly and comprehensively.

In preparing a speech, another frequently encountered problem is where to find appropriate humorous or poignant material. We personally found that while there were books of anecdotes for public speakers, the majority of this material was inappropriate when applied to educational topics. Consequently, we began keeping our own "story file." If we heard or came across something that applied to an aspect of education, and it was truly good, we would file it for later use in public speaking. This was material that came not only from books, but from teachers, from the classroom, from the school, from the interplay between student and teacher, parent and child, faculty and administrator, from those real-life situations which make us smile and somehow make the day a little shorter and the burdens a little lighter.

What we collected consisted of material to which our audience of educators could relate, material which struck familiar and responsive chords, which engendered the chuckle, the laugh, the nod of the head which said, in not so many words—we are pleased; we are happy; we understand.

And that material forms the basis of this book. Complete with encyclopedic headings, this book covers every aspect of education. From kindergarten to the college classroom, from frantic parents to the philosophies of poets, from the writings of students to the remembrances of teachers—you will find all of these and more within the pages of this complete library of educational wit and humor.

Nor must you use it only for a speech. Use it in your classroom; use it in the teacher's room; use it at your next faculty meeting; your next conference. Get someone to laugh with you, and you have undermined any barriers to communication that may have existed.

This book is an inexhaustible gold mine of audience-tested material. Every entry has been polished and refined to provide wit, humor, dignity and entertainment value for both you and your audience. Make no mistake—this is not merely a series of jokes meant for a stand-up comedian. Rather, this is a complete and thorough compendium of material especially prepared for you, the professional educator, to enliven and enrich your speeches.

Finally, it is inevitable that problems will occur in public speaking. They are not, however, insurmountable and may, quite often, be turned to the speaker's advantage. Therefore, we have included "WHAT DO YOU DO IF . . . A Troubleshooter's Handy Guide to Every Speaking Occasion," an invaluable resource which allows you to draw upon the experience of your fellow educators in efficiently handling those "special" problems.

One man we knew, for example, was considered a fine speaker, except when it came time for him to take questions from the floor. Often he would become flustered, stammer, or give half-answers, leaving the audience with the impression that he was unsure of himself and his material. Such was not the case, and once he learned the A*R*E*A formula of question response, he was able to prove it. Now, when questions come his way, he is decisive, informative, and projects strength to his audience.

In Part II you will find the A*R*E*A formula, along with invaluable, specific answers and guidelines on what to do if your audience is tired and restless, if your speech is interrupted, if you are not feeling well, and many, many more.

Educator's Lifetime Library of Stories, Quotes, Anecdotes, Wit and Humor is truly a book to use—over and over and over again. This is not a book that will gather dust, for you will delve into its encyclopedic depths time and again in order to enliven your classroom; to "break the ice" at conferences and in-service training sessions; to establish a congenial, receptive atmosphere at the next faculty meeting; to add just the "right" touch of humor to your next speech; to insure your success as a memorable Master of Ceremonies; to avoid problems and to successfully handle those problems if and when they do occur; or just to read and chuckle to yourself. The combination of its many uses, the thoroughness and completeness of its contents, and the laugh-filled, entertaining, audience-tested nature of the material it contains, will make it a welcome and *practical* addition to any educator's library.

P. Susan Mamchak

Steven R. Mamchak

Acknowledgments

We are grateful to those who granted permission to use portions of material from other sources. A detailed list follows, indicating appropriate credit and the particular entry numbers involved in each case. The absence of any reference to the origin of a particularly entry indicates the original source is unknown. Our sincere appreciation is extended to those who permitted use of the following material:

Copyright © 1970 by Arlington House, New Rochelle, New York. Taken from *Quotations from Chairman Bill*. All rights reserved. Used with permission. **189, 234, 248, 738.**

John Mason Brown, *Accustomed as I Am*, by permission of Manufacturer's Hanover Trust Company and Catherine Meredith Brown, as trustees under the will of John Mason Brown. **246, 988.**

Citadel Press, Inc., *The Algonquin Wits* by Robert E. Brennan, New York, 1968. Used with permission. **49, 468, 758.**

From *Thought Starters* by Ted Cook, Copyright © 1967 by Ted Cook, published by Abelard-Schuman, Ltd., Publisher. **63, 160, 161, 236, 554, 748.**

From *Here Are My Lectures* by Stephen Leacock, Dodd, Mead & Company, New York. **247, 491, 917, 930.**

From *Grab a Pencil, No. 2*, Copyright 1970, Hart Publishing Company, Inc. **83, 92, 192, 305, 329, 357, 379, 392, 393, 439, 440, 560, 561, 603, 604, 625, 627, 678, 702, 730, 736, 905, 957.**

Reprinted by permission of Hawthorn Books, Inc., from *The Funniest Jokes and How to Tell Them* by Mark Wachs, Copyright © Hawthorn Books, 1968. All rights reserved. **98, 101, 119, 173, 229, 275, 283, 365, 445, 450, 476, 507, 663.**

TABLE OF CONTENTS

Part I

EDUCATOR'S LIFETIME LIBRARY
of
Stories, Quotes, Anecdotes, Wit and Humor

Absent-Minded

1. "What did you do with the car?" asked the professor's wife.

"I'm sorry," remarked the professor quizically, "but did I take the car with me this morning?"

"You certainly did. You drove it to the campus."

"Now I remember!" exclaimed the professor. "It did strike me as odd that the man who had given me a lift drove off before I could thank him!"

2. Then there was the professor who was so absent-minded that he couldn't take a shower because he could never find the pocket in which he had left the soap.

3. At the reunion, the professor was complaining to an alumnus whom he had just met.

"I have a student named Jones," he said, "who is the laziest, most good-for-nothing, undisciplined . . ."

"Henry!" whispered one of his colleagues, "You've done it again. Don't you remember? That's the boy's father!"

". . . but then," continued the professor without hesitation, "every great man has had his faults."

4.   As the professor corrected his class's mid-term exams, his wife burst into the room angrily waving the college newspaper.

"Just look at this!" she shouted. "They've announced your death on the front page!"

"Why bother me," said the professor without looking up. "Just send flowers and a note of condolence."

Absenteeism

5.   Of course, there was the absentee who claimed the reason he had played hooky was that his mind had wandered, and he followed it.

6.   Tommy was absent on the day his mother gave birth to twins. When he returned home from school on the following day, his father asked him if his teacher had accepted his excuse, and what she had thought about the twins.

"Yep! And she was real pleased about my baby brother."

"Brother? You mean brother *and* sister, don't you?"

"Nope! I only told her about one. I figure the other one will be good for a day off next Wednesday when we have a test."

7.   Jamie claimed the reason he was absent was that he knew he would be very late, so he decided not to come at all.

"But if you were going to be late," asked his teacher, "why didn't you just start earlier?"

"It was too late to start earlier," was his reply.

Achievement

8. Stand up and be counted, or be counted among the missing.

9. "Son," said Johnny's father, "according to this report card, you're at the bottom of your class, and I'm really worried that you're not getting a proper education."

"That's O.K., Dad," answered Johnny. "Don't you know they teach the same thing at both ends?"

10. The Russian father was bragging to his comrade.

"My sons are very successful. Why, one of them is a People's Doctor, another is a People's Engineer, and a third is a People's Commissar. But the one who has achieved the most is the one who defected to America."

"Oh," said the comrade, "and what does he do in America?"

"It's a very important job. He stands on something called an Unemployment Line, and believe me, if it weren't for the money he sends home, we'd all starve."

11. There is nothing that the mind of man can conceive that he cannot achieve if he is willing to pay the price. That price is time.

Adolescence-Adolescent

12. Put the personality of a child in the body of a man, furnish a need to be loved and a fierce desire to be independent, allow a need to be self-directing but leave out any idea of what direction to take, add an enormous amount of love but also the fear that it may not be accepted or returned, give physical and sexual powers without any knowledge or experience of how to use them—take these and place them in a society whose values and achievements are essentially incomprehensible and certainly unattainable and whose concerns are seemingly misplaced and insincere. Then you have just begun to understand the problems of adolescence.

13.   Many a teenaged boy will tell you that adolescence is the time when a girl's voice changes from "no" to "yes."

14.   The difference between adolescence and middle-age is that in adolescence you are absolutely positive that you will live forever, while in middle age you're merely grateful that you've lasted as long as you have.

15.   Over the course of a lifetime, a person usually goes from wide-eyed idealism to cautious conservatism. The difficulty in dealing with the adolescent arises from the fact that while they are in the former stage, their parents are in the latter.

16.   Adolescence changes to adulthood on the day when a son, arm-wrestling with his father, suddenly discovers that he can win, looks into the old man's face, and let's his father beat him.

17.   Adolescent: Someone who will gladly spend twenty dollars for a new shirt and then staunchly refuse to use a twenty-cent hanger.

Adult Education

18.   What need did our parents have for Adult Education? They had a bunch of kids—that was enough!

19.   Adult Education is a strenuous effort to learn something that bored you to death when you were still young enough to have used it.

Adults

20.   At the faculty Christmas party, a certain teacher had imbibed a bit too much. Returning home, he was determined not to allow his wife to discover his condition.

Entering his home, he found his wife entertaining the next door neighbor and her newborn twins.

Gazing at the two babies, the teacher drew himself up to his full height and in the soberest voice he could manage proclaimed, "Well, well, that *is* a beautiful baby."

21. An adult is a person who has stopped growing up and down and has started to grow from side to side.

22. Johnny was overjoyed the day he received his driver's license, and began to extoll the virtues of modern transportation to Grandma.

"Just imagine," Johnny continued. "I can take my date anywhere. Why, if we wanted to go to a movie fifty miles away, we could do it. Don't you wish you could have traveled like that when you were dating?"

"I don't know," said Grandma with a twinkle in her eye. "As I recall, we went about as far as we could."

Advice

23. The brand new teacher and the veteran educator were talking.

"Sir," said the new teacher, "do you have any advice for me before I step into the classroom?"

"Son," answered the veteran, "if there is anything that my years of experience have taught me it's that in almost every class there'll be a student ready for an argument. Your first impulse will be to silence him, but think carefully before doing so. He may be the only one who has been paying attention."

24. The business teacher advised the office aide that she must always be able to find something when the principal calls for it.

"Therefore," the teacher concluded, "you'd better brush up on your filing skills."

The office aide turned out to be one of the most efficient the school ever had.

"Well," congratulated the teacher, "I see you took my advice about filing."

"I sure did," answered the student. "And it's so much simpler than you taught us in class. I just make twenty-six copies of everything and file one under each letter!"

25.   Frank Lloyd Wright, the noted architect, reportedly gave some advice that we all can follow.

Wright recalled how he was awakened one night by a frantic telephone call from a client whose house had just recently been completed.

It seems that it had been raining, the roof leaked, and the living room was flooded. "What should I do?" asked the distraught client.

Calmly, Frank Lloyd Wright replied, "Rise above it."

26.   The ancient sage who first advised, "Know Thyself," would have been pleased with the mother who told her daughter on the occasion of the girl's first "big" date, "Dear, 'no' thyself."

27.   "Mom," ran the telegram from the co-ed, "Have big date. Has seen all my clothes. Send fifty dollars for new dress. Love, Pam."

Came the reply: "Pam: Am sending five dollars. Get new *boy*. Love, Mom."

28.   "Ma'am," asked the kindergarten student, "do you have any kids of your own?"

"No," replied the teacher. "I've asked God for children, but so far I haven't been blessed with any."

"Excuse me, Ma'am," said the tyke, "but shouldn't you ask your husband, too?"

29.   "Won't you say a few words to the class?" the teacher asked the politician who was touring the school.

"Certainly," he smiled. "I wonder if any of you lovely little boys and girls could give me some advice on what I should talk about since I have nothing prepared to say?"

One small hand waved in the back of the room.

"If I were you," said the tiny voice, "I'd shut my mouth and let us get on with recess!"

30.   As the new principal was cleaning out the old principal's desk, he found three sealed letters, each bearing the legend, "To The New Principal," the first stating, "Open During Your First Crisis," the next stating, "Open During Your Second Crisis," and the final one stating, "Open During Your Third Crisis."

It wasn't long before a crisis arose, and the new principal went to his desk and opened the first letter.

It read, "Plead ignorance."

Following this advice, the principal stated that he was unfamiliar with the case, had just been appointed, etc., and the crisis passed.

Presently, a second crisis arose, and opening the appropriate envelope the principal read, "Ask for more time."

He did just that, and sure enough, the crisis passed.

Finally, there arose a crisis from which the principal could see no escape. Eagerly, he ran to his office, extracted the last envelope from his desk, tore it open, and spread the paper before him.

The letter began, "First, write three letters . . ."

Age Levels

31.   While standing before a reconstructed dinosaur skeleton during a field trip to a local museum, the teacher asked her charges, "Does anyone know how old these bones are?"

"I do," volunteered Timmy. "They're exactly one hundred fifty million and one years old."

"How can you be so exact?" asked his teacher.

"That's easy," answered Timmy. "My mother told me they were one hundred and fifty million years old, and that was when she brought me here last year."

32.   "If a person were born in 1950," asked the teacher, "how old would that person be today?"

"That all depends," piped up Tommy.

"On what?"

"Well, it depends on whether it's a he-person or a she-person."

33.   It is said that mankind goes through three ages: Youth, Middle Age, and "Doesn't he look good, considering . . ."

34.   Not only are children an aid and comfort in your old age, but, as any parent will tell you, having them is the quickest way to get there!

35.   It sort of makes you wonder when senior citizens are given free passes to amusement parks while teenagers are asked to evaluate Foreign Policy.

36.   When the co-ed told her father that she had become engaged, the doting parent stammered, "But . . . but, you're only twenty-one, and he's almost thirty. I don't see why you can't wait a few years until you catch up with him!"

37.   The age you hope to reach is always ten years older than you are.

38.   "Your son," wrote home the Nursery School Teacher, "is immature."

Wrote back the mother: "He is four years old. If he can't be immature now, what age would you suggest?"

39.   "When I was your age," admonished the father, "I could name every state in the Union."

"So what," said Johnny. "Anybody can memorize thirteen names!"

40. A sixth-grade teacher was trying to impress upon her class the rigors of Valley Forge. As she conjured up pictures of the biting cold and heavy snows, the children sat enthralled.

"All this," she concluded, "took place over two-hundred years ago."

Wow, Miss Jones!" exclaimed one of her charges. "You sure have *some* memory."

Allowance

41. One of the first things a kid learns in school is how to ask for a bigger allowance.

42. "Dad, can I have five dollars?"

"Dollars? Dollars? Why when I was a kid I was content to have *dimes*."

"O.K., I'll take it in dimes."

Alumni

43. "If I had my life to live over," said the high-school principal, "I'd run an orphanage. Then I wouldn't have to contend with the P.T.A."

"Not me," said his friend, the college president. "I'd be a prison warden. Have you ever heard of *their* alumni forming pressure groups?"

44. The day after the reunion, a somewhat bleary-eyed participant was explaining to the college president what had caused the extensive damage to the rose garden.

"Believe me, Sir," the old grad continued, "no alumni did that. It was a drunk from *town*."

America

45. You never know what patriotism means until someone from another country wins the gold medal.

46. America is the only country on earth where defendants are let loose while the jury is locked up.

47. At the graduation exercises from citizenship school, the principal began to ask the new Americans why they had chosen to become citizens.

"I love democracy," said the native Russian.

"I came for the economic opportunities," replied the ex-Brazilian.

"Well, you see," began the former British subject, "I've always wanted to *win* the Revolutionary War . . ."

48. "Maria," called her husband, "our citizenship papers have arrived. We are now Americans."

"Are you sure we are Americans?" she asked.

"I am sure."

"Are you positive we are Americans?"

"I'm positive."

"Are you absolutely certain we are Americans?"

"Maria, I am telling you that we are now Americans!"

"In that case, get your feet off the couch and take out the garbage."

Animals

49. A dog teaches a boy fidelity, perseverance, and how to turn around three times before lying down.

—Robert Bencnly

50.   While the first-grade class was on its Nature Walk, a deer bounded into a nearby clearing.

"Oh, look!" exclaimed the teacher. "Bobby, can you tell the class what kind of animal that is?"

"I don't know."

"Of course you do," chided the teacher. "I'll give you a hint: What does your Mommy call your Daddy?"

"Gee!" gasped Bobby. "So that's what a skunk looks like."

51.   One little boy cracked up his first-grade teacher with this one: "Miss Stanley, can I bring a raccoon to school?"

"A raccoon? Well . . . that all depends. Is it dead or alive?"

"I don't know, but my Daddy says that if we wait awhile it'll turn into a butterfly."

52.   The teacher returned home one day to find his small daughter in tears. It seems that "Sam," her pet lizard, had passed away.

"Don't cry," said the father, mentally reviewing his knowledge of child psychology. "I'll tell you what, let's have a funeral for Sam."

With the aid of paint, paste, and paper, a cigar box was turned into an elegant coffin. A hole was dug in the back yard, and a hand-made "tombstone" was placed at its head. With somber music playing on the phonograph, and the entire family assembled, the father spoke glowingly of "Sam's" past life and devotion.

"Gee, Daddy,'" sniffled the little girl, "this is beautiful."

Just then, "Sam" twitched his tail and began to move about.

The little girl looked first at "Sam," then at the funeral arrangements, and finally at her father.

"Hey, Dad," she whispered, "What d'ya say we kill him?"

53.   "I know how baby kittens are made," announced the kindergarten youngster.

"Oh," said the teacher warily. "How?"

"There's nothing to it. The mama cat walks into a closet and falls apart."

54. "Billy," said Mother, "where is your gerbil?"

"I don't know, Mom," answered Billy. "I haven't seen him since I vacuum-cleaned his cage."

Art

55. Art, like morality, consists in drawing the line somewhere.

—G. K. Chesterton

56. As the art student sketched his girlfriend, he couldn't resist the urge to bend forward and kiss her.

"Well," she said jealously. "And do you kiss all your models?"

"Of course not," he replied indignantly. "I've had three other models, and you're the only one I've kissed."

"And do I know these other models?"

"I don't think so," replied the student. "The first was a chair, the second was a lamp, and the third was a basket of fruit."

57. "I hope," said the principal to the art teacher, "that you don't intend to show your class any examples of abstract painting."

"But, why shouldn't I?"

"Really, Miss Thomas," proclaimed the principal. "With abstract painting it's impossible to tell which pictures are risqué and which are morally correct!"

Assemblies

58. "Students," said the principal at the assembly, "I have some good news and some bad news for you. First, the good news is that this morning we will have half a day of school."

"And what's the bad news?" shouted a student from the audience.

"The bad news is that we'll have the other half of the day this afternoon!"

Automobiles

59. Why is it that each year it takes less and less time to fly from coast to coast and more and more time to drive to school each morning?

60. Three of the major problems in today's high schools are teachers' salaries, relevant curriculum, and finding enough parking spaces for the students' cars.

61. The teacher had taken her full-sized car downtown to do some shopping. The only parking space available was one in which she would have to parallel park in very tight quarters. As she began the arduous task of backing in, she noticed two of her fourth-grade charges watching her intently from the corner.

Taking a deep breath, she proceeded to park beautifully on the first attempt, without even touching a bumper.

As she got out, one of the students came forward and put a nickel in the parking meter.

"Tommy," she said, "you didn't have to do that."

"Yes, I did, Ma'am," answered Tommy. "I lost fair and square."

—Martha Greenwald

62. An elementary and a secondary school teacher were discussing the relative merits of their positions.

"In high school," said the one, "I don't have to walk the students to the bus. Most of them drive themselves."

"True," answered the other. "But then, in elementary school *I'm* always sure of a place to park."

Awards

63. When the old teacher passed away, there was much mourning on the part of his former students.

"He has gone to his reward," they moaned.

Years later, when one of those students was also called, he arrived in heaven and requested that he be taken to his old teacher.

He found the old man reclining on a fluffy cloud, being fed grapes by a voluptuous and shapely young lady.

"Professor," said the former student, "I am just overjoyed to see you rewarded in this manner."

"You still haven't learned to think," the professor chided. "Can't you see that she's not *my* reward? I'm *her* punishment!"

64. "What did you get that medal for?" asked Willie's mother as she picked up his jacket from the floor.

"I got it in school," he replied as he dropped a jelly sandwich on the living room rug.

"I know," she said as she stumbled over the shoes he had left in the middle of the hallway. "But what is it for?"

Willy answered with a smile: "Neatness!"

Baby-Sitting

65. "I'm so sorry we're late," apologized little Johnny's parents, "but the car broke down, and we . . ."

"That's O.K.,". interrupted the frazzled baby sitter as she brushed a loose strand of hair from her face. "If he were my child, I wouldn't be anxious to come home either."

66. "Excuse me," the star quarterback said to the freshman co-ed, "didn't I see you at the last football game?"

"You sure did," she sighed.

"I hope you won't think this forward of me, but are you doing anything this evening?"

"Why no, not a thing," she gulped.

"Gee, that's great. Can I ask you something?"

"Go right ahead," she murmured.

"Well," he said, "my wife and I have to attend a football banquet, and I was wondering if you could baby-sit for our little boy?"

67. "Why do you think you're such a good babysitter?" asked the mother.

"Well, for one thing, I never mind when babies cry," said the teenage girl.

"And why is that?"

"It's a matter of philosophy, Ma'am," explained the baby sitter. "I just figure that if I were bald, didn't have any teeth, and couldn't stand up by myself, I'd be crying, too."

Baseball

68. The father arrived late to an after-school ball game.

"What's the score, Jerry?" he asked his son.

"It's nineteen to zero against us, Pop."

"That's terrible, son, but at least you don't sound discouraged."

"Why should I be?" returned the boy. "We haven't even been up yet."

69. An umpire may be defined as the original strike arbitrator.

Basketball

70. "I understand," admonished the basketball coach, "that some of you have been talking rather freely and giving away our secret plays. That has to stop. I want you to be silent. I want you to be absolutely mute!"

"What did he say?" whispered a late arrival to a teammate.

"He says he wants a mutiny," came the answer.

71. "What a night I had last night," said the basketball coach. "What happened?" asked his colleague.

"I had a blind date with this gorgeous redhead, and we no sooner met than she invited me to her home. When we got there, she fixed us drinks, put soft music on the stereo, and turned the lights down low. That's when it happened."

"What? What?"

"Her brother walked in, he was seven feet tall, and I talked him into coming here next semester!"

Behavior

72. Little Freddy slammed open the door, barreled down the hall, knocking down his baby sister in the process, and thundered into the living room, upsetting the coffee table and breaking one of the table lamps.

"Good grief, Freddy!" exclaimed his mother. "What on earth is the matter?"

"We got our report cards today, Mom," he panted, "and I got an 'A'—in Behavior."

73. "Darling," said the mother, "don't you know that every time you misbehave, you put another wrinkle on your Mommy's face."

"Aha!" said the child. "So you're the reason Grandma looks like that!"

74. THE PERFECT CHILD

It asked for bread and butter first,
It ceased to eat before it burst.
It kept its clothing clean and neat,
It blew its nose, it wiped its feet.
Meekly repentant when it erred,
Was seldom seen and never heard.
Ordered itself with zeal intense
To those of ripened years and sense.

It walked demurely through the land
With governesses hand in hand.
It fled from rowdy little boys,
It turned from vulgar books and toys,
From pantomimes and such distractions,
And gave its time to vulgar fractions.
But when it takes to married life
I shall be sorry for its wife!

—*Adrian Porter*

75. "Well, Tim," said the boy's mother, "I hope you were a good boy in school today."

"I sure was," responded Timmy. "After all, you can't get in much trouble when you're sitting in the principal's office."

76. The teacher returned to the class she had momentarily left and found the students seated quietly at their desks, hands folded, watching her intently. This lasted for about ten seconds, and then the class let out a collective sigh of disappointment.

"What is it?" the teacher demanded. "What's the matter?"

"Gosh, Miss Thompson," volunteered one student. "You said yesterday that if you ever came into this room and found us well behaved, you'd faint. Well, we were, but you didn't!"

77. On the first day of school, one young boy rushed to open the door for an arriving teacher.

"Why, thank you. I'm not used to such good manners," said the teacher. "It's a very pleasant surprise."

"I'm sorry I startled you," said the boy, "but I'm a new student, and I don't know any better."

78. "Boy, Dad, my teacher is really interested in you."

"How do you know that, son?"

"Well, today, right after I threw the spitball at the principal, I heard her say, 'What must his father be like?' "

79. It is not enough to believe in what is right; not only must one believe it—one must behave it!

80. "Of course my son has a reason for his misbehavior, and it's an excellent reason. He didn't know you were watching him."

81. Behavior is quite often a matter of point of view. Should three people perform the same act, *I'd* be rational, *you* would be peculiar, and *the other guy* would be totally illogical.

82. "Class!" shouted the distraught teacher at her fourth-grade students. "I want you to come to order this minute. I won't have this behavior. You're acting like children!"

Biology

83. From a biology test paper: "A corps is a dead gentleman; a corpse is a dead lady."

84. From another biology test paper: "The smallest veins in your body are called caterpillars."

85. "Mom, where's the thread?"
"What do you want with the thread?"
"Well, our biology teacher told us that our genes make us what we are, and mine have a hole in them."

86. "Remember," said the biology teacher, "every human being is composed of over ninety percent water."
Just then, a shapely co-ed passed by the classroom door.
"Man," said one student to another, "that's what I call making waves!"

Board of Education

87.   In the first place God made idiots. This was for practice. Then He made school boards.

—Mark Twain

88.   A Board of Education is a group that keeps minutes and wastes hours.

89.   The parents' meeting adjourned with an announcement by the principal that there would be a meeting of the Board in a few moments.

"That's for me," said one parent to another. "I'm at least as bored as anybody else here."

90.   "What does a person do," ran the homework question, "when he or she is running for the Board?"

Johnny, with faultless fifth-grade logic, wrote: "They run very hard until they catch it, and then they sit on it."

Books

91.   The man who does not read good books has no advantage over the man who can't read them.

—Mark Twain

92.   "Our teacher said she was a 'bibliomaniac.' I wonder what that means?" asked one youngster.

"Simple," replied another youngster. "That just means she reads the Bible from cover to cover."

93. The student approached the school librarian's desk, and began to scratch her head in obvious perplexity.

"I want to take out a book," she said. "I think the title is *The Red Boat.*"

"I'm sorry," said the librarian, "but I don't recognize that title."

"Maybe I made a mistake. Do you have a book called *The Scarlet Launch?*"

"Do you mean *The Scarlet Letter* by Hawthorne?"

"No, I'm positive it had something to do with ships."

"Well, I'm sorry, but I don't see how . . ."

"Now I remember!" shouted the student. "I want *The Ruby Yacht* by a Mr. Omar!"

94. In preparation for the visit of a rambunctious two-year-old, all fragile objects were moved to higher ground.

As the doorbell rang, the daughter whispered, "Mom, what about the Bible? Do you want me to move that, too?"

"Never mind, Dear," answered the Mother. "The only things breakable in there are the Ten Commandments."

Botany

95. The teacher asked her kindergarten students, "Who can tell me how to find out what is a weed and what is a flower?"

"I know," volunteered a precocious six-year-old. "You pull up everything, and if it still comes up—it's a weed."

96. "Miss," said the teenage boy to the florist, "I'm looking for a flower that will tell my girl exactly what I think of her."

"How about a dozen American Beauty roses?" suggested the florist. "That would only be eighteen dollars."

"Gosh," gulped the boy. "That's a little high. Do you have a Local Cutie for about five dollars?"

Boys

97. Have you ever noticed that a boy can unwrap a candy bar while holding a sweater, a baseball and bat, and three books, and yet can't put a garbage cover on straight with two hands?

98. To a young boy there is no such time as "between meals."

Brothers and Sisters

99. "If your mother gave you a large piece of cake and a small piece of cake and told you to give one to your brother," the teacher asked, "which would you give him?"

"That depends," said little Alan. "Is it my big brother or my little brother?"

100. "I really put my teacher in a good mood today, Dad."

"Oh, and how did you manage that?"

"Simple. I told her I was an only child."

101. Mother dashed into the nursery when she heard her five-year-old howling. His baby sister, it developed, was pulling his hair.

"Never mind," she comforted. "Your little sister doesn't know that it hurts you."

A few minutes later, Mother had to come back to the nursery. This time, the baby was howling.

"What's the matter with the baby?" she demanded.

"Nothing much," replied the five-year-old calmly. "Only now *she* knows."

102. The teacher called the first grader to one side.

"Donna," she began, "I heard some of the other children talking, and they were saying that you gave your little brother a present. Is that true?"

"Yes, Ma'am."

"Well I think that's just fine, and unselfish, and ever so nice of you. And what was it that you gave him?"

Came the smiling reply: "Chicken Pox!"

103. The teacher was explaining the characteristics of serpents to her second grade class.

"So you see," she concluded, "a snake is an unlikeable creature that crawls on the ground and causes trouble wherever it goes. Now, can anyone use the word 'snake' correctly in a sentence?"

One hand shot up.

"I know," said Billy. " 'My baby sister is a perfect snake!' "

104. The eighth grade Safety Patrol brought two disheveled first graders back to their teacher.

"They were fighting on the playground," said the older boy. "I got their names, and do you know what? They aren't even related! Boy, the way they were going at it, I'd have sworn they were brothers!"

Bus Driver, The School

105. The postman was making a delivery to a local church, and stepped inside to hand the mail to the pastor. All at once the doors of the church crashed open, and an obviously distraught man rushed in, ran down the aisle, and threw himself at the foot of the altar. The man wept copiously, beat his fists on the floor, turned his face imploringly to heaven, and finally collapsed in a heap, moaning softly.

"A repentant sinner?" whispered the mailman.

"Not at all," answered the pastor. "That's Mr. Jones. He drives a school bus, and he's just completed his morning run."

106. Anyone who drives a school bus for any length of time is a person who *used* to like children.

107. "I can always tell when one of the boys has reached that awkward age," claimed the school bus driver. "He stands in the aisle, and he can't make up his mind if he should offer a girl his seat or arm-wrestle her for it."

108. Fortunately, the school bus was empty when the oncoming car swerved left, swerved right, and finally exchanged paint with the bus as it passed.

The school bus driver scrambled out of the bus, surveyed the damage, and angrily approached the driver of the offending vehicle.

"Madam!" roared the bus driver. "Why didn't you signal which way you were going?"

"Don't be silly," shrugged the woman. "How could I signal when I hadn't even made up my mind?"

109. With all the troubles faced by the school bus driver, it is a wonder that they are as patient as they are.

"It's all a matter of philosophy," said one driver to his colleague. "Each morning I get on that bus and I say to myself, 'You are happy; the children are a joy; and this is a fine way to make a living.' And it works! I do feel happy and alive. Actually, there's only one drawback to the whole thing."

"And what is that?"

"I can only lie to myself for the first trip!"

Business Education

110. As an assignment for the Junior Business Training class, the teacher had asked each student to define "ethics" as it applied to business.

One boy sought the aid of his father, a prominent local businessman, who told him: "Perhaps an example will help. This afternoon I waited on a customer at the store who paid for his purchase with a twenty-dollar bill. After he had left, I was fingering the money, and it separated in my hands. The man had given me *two* twenty-dollar bills stuck together as one. Now, here's where ethics and business come together. Do I or do I not tell my partner?"

111. "Let us suppose," said the business teacher, "that you owned some land bordered on one side by the town dump, on another side by a sewage plant, on a third side by an oil refinery, and on a fourth side by a pig farm. How would you go about selling this property?"

"That's easy," replied a boy whose father worked in real estate, "I'd sell it to the Weather Bureau."

"Why would the Weather Bureau want that land?" asked the teacher.

"Simple. I'd just make them aware that if they settled there, they wouldn't need any fancy instruments to know which way the wind was blowing."

112. "My father says that business is terrible," said the student.

"Come, now, Johnny," replied the business teacher, "I drive past your father's motel every afternoon, and there's always a 'No Vacancy' sign in the window."

"That doesn't mean a thing," replied the boy. "Why, my father says we used to not have room for forty couples, and now we're lucky if we turn away twenty!"

Cafeteria

113. "I'm bringing my lunch from now on," the little boy informed his mother. "I ain't gonna eat that cafeteria food no more! They serve *sick food*!"

"What do you mean, 'sick food'?"

"Well, today I looked in one of the ovens, and they were roasting a chicken, and it was sick. I know, 'cause it had a thermometer in it!"

114. "Coach!" yelled the student, running up, "We can't have the baseball game today. Some vandals broke into the locker room and stole the bases!"

"Quick," said the coach, handing the boy some money, "run to the cafeteria and buy four pancakes!"

115. "Something terrible has happened!" the cafeteria worker informed the vice-principal. "Someone broke into the cafeteria and ate the meatloaf!"

"Calm down," advised the vice-principal. "We'll organize a search for the body."

116. The history teacher had been assigned cafeteria duty. On his first day he noticed a boy throwing away a salad.

"Son," he admonished, "if George Washington had had that salad at Valley Forge, he'd have eaten it."

"I know," said the boy, "but it was probably fresh then."

117. "This is not going to be my day," said the student to his friend.

"How do you figure that?"

"Well," he replied, "I failed the algebra test, got caught passing a note in class, and worst of all, I left my lunch at home, and the cafeteria is serving spinach!"

118. While trying to explain proper nutrition, the health teacher asked a student, "If you went down to our cafeteria and were served a meal consisting of fresh fruit, delicious vegetables, juicy steak, cold milk, and a tempting desert, what would you be having?"

Replied the student: "A dream."

Chauvinism

119. Said the nursery school boy to the nursery school girl: "Are you the opposite sex or am I?"

120. After the first day of second grade, the two friends met on the school bus.

"I think I'm gonna like this year," said Tommy.

"Not me," said Alan.

"Why not?"

"Have you *seen* my class?" Alan lamented. "We got six boys and ten thousand girls!"

121. The world is packed with good women. To know them is a middle-class education.

—Oscar Wilde

122. The two tourists bumped into each other on a busy street in Paris.

"What country do you come from?" asked the gentleman from the United States.

"I come from the greatest country on the face of the earth!" stated the Russian.

"Funny," said the other. "You don't *sound* like an American."

123. Little Mary stood up in Sunday School class.

"God made Adam," she said, "and that was the first man."

"Correct," stated the teacher. "Now what about Eve?"

"Oh, yes. Well, after Adam had been around for a while, God said, 'Boy, I could really improve on this model . . .' "

124. It was the little girl's first time at a ski resort. Try as she might, she could not seem to master the beginner's slope.

"Boys ski better than girls," her brother stated as he glided up to her.

"Maybe so," she said calmly, "but I bet they mind falling down more."

Chemistry

125. "If you had to list the ten greatest contributions that chemistry has made to mankind," said the professor, "what would you include?"

The student thought a while and then answered: "I think first would come blonds . . ."

126.   There was a young student named Bell,
            Who always used NaCl.
            A mistake made him pour
            H_2SO_4
            On his food—Now he don't feel so well.

Children

127. The only thing children wear out faster than clothes are parents.

128. It is one of the paradoxes of life that we spend the first couple years of our children's lives trying to get them to talk, and then we spend the rest of their childhood trying to get them to shut up.

129. Whatever you would have your children become, strive to exhibit in your own lives and conversations.

                                        —*Lydia Huntley Sigourney*

130. Little Jane was complaining about the difficulty of her acting assignment in the Sunday School Christmas play.
      "Honestly, Mother," she stated, "you have no idea how hard it is to be a virgin!"

131. The nicest thing about children is that *they* don't pull out a wallet filled with pictures of their parents!

132. Little Mark prayed for snow in order that he might use his new sled. When he awoke the next morning, flakes of white were battering his window pane.

Dressing quickly and running outside, he looked skyward and exclaimed, "That's the idea, God! Keep it coming!"

133. Two mothers were discussing the virtues of their teenage sons.

"My son," said one, "pays for his own clothes."

"That's nothing," said the other. "My son pays his own psychiatrist's bill!"

134. After listening to their daughter beg and plead for one of those new dolls that does *everything,* her parents decided to get her one for her birthday.

They listened patiently while the toy dealer explained how the doll wets, cries, dribbles, coos, speaks ten languages, has a 52-page instruction manual, and only costs half a king's ransom.

Turning to his wife, the husband implored, "Wouldn't it be easier if we just gave her a baby sister?"

135. Children are like Mexican jumping beans as anyone will tell you who has ever tried to keep one down.

136. "You teachers are so lucky to be able to work with children," said the P.T.A. president. "Why, I'd give a year of my life just to be able to teach for one week."

"At least she has the proper rate of exchange," commented a teacher.

Choices

137. There was a wise man who was much beloved by the people of his country. There was also an evil Prince who hated the wise man for having the affection of the people while he, the Prince, did not. The Prince sought constantly to discredit the wise man. Finally, he hit upon a plan.

"Tomorrow," said the Prince, "when the wise man goes to

the market place to talk to the people, I shall be there. I will hold a
dove in my hand, and I will say, 'Wise Man! Tell me—this bird
which I hold in my hand—is it alive or is it dead?' If he says it is
dead, I will open my hand and let the bird fly away. If he says it is
alive, I will crush the dove in my hand and let it fall to the ground,
dead. Either way I will have made the wise man appear a fool!''

The next day came, and the Prince was at the market place
before the wise man arrived. He waited patiently, and when the wise
man appeared and began speaking, the Prince took the dove from its
cage and raised his voice above the crowd.

"Wise Man!'' he shouted, "I would ask you a simple question:
This bird which I hold in my hand—is it alive or is it dead?''

The crowd grew silent, and all eyes turned toward the wise
man. The wise man paused, looked first at the people and then at the
Prince, and said: "That which you hold in your hand, it is . . . what
you make of it.''

138.   When the student stubbed his toe, a professor directed him
to the college infirmary. Upon entering the place, the student found
himself confronted by two doors, one marked *Illness* and the other
marked *Trauma.* Figuring that a bump was a trauma, he chose that
door and was immediately confronted by two more doors, one with
the title *Internal* and the other with *External.* He concluded that a
bump on the toe was external, and went through that door. Again,
there were two doors, this time marked *Serious* and *Minor.* Walking
through the door marked *Minor,* he suddenly found himself back out
on the campus.

"Did they take care of your toe?'' asked the professor.

"No, they didn't,'' said the student, "but man, are they ever
organized!''

139.   A father took his teenage daughter shopping.

"You're old enough now to choose your own clothes,'' he
said. "Go into that store and pick out any dress you like. I'll be back
to pick you up in a week.''

140.   The centipede was happy quite
'Til said a toad in fun,
"How choose you which leg goes with which?"
That worked her mind to such a pitch,
She lay distracted in a ditch,
Considering how to run.

—E. Craster

Citizenship

141. What is the worth of a single vote? Consider:
Thomas Jefferson was elected President by one vote in the electoral college. So was John Quincy Adams. Rutherford B. Hayes was elected President by one vote. His election was contested; referred to an electoral commission where the matter was again decided by a single vote. The man who cast the deciding vote for President Hayes was himself elected to Congress by the margin of one vote. California, Washington, Idaho, Texas, and Oregon gained statehood by one vote, and the War of 1812 was brought about by a series of events based upon one vote.

142. With everything you read in the newspapers, it does you good if you stop and realize that last year there were over thirty million of our youth who were *not* taken into custody by the police for any reason.

143. A teacher was overheard discussing the citizenship of one of her students.
"He comes from a good home," she said. "He has a fine peer relationship, an above average I.Q., and no emotional hang-ups. He's just a pain in the neck!"

144. When a dog wandered into the kindergarten class, one tyke asked loudly, "Is it a boy-dog or a girl-dog?"

Before the teacher could answer, another child burst in with, "I know how we can tell."

As the teacher sputtered nervously, the lad continued, "Let's have a vote!"

Classroom

145.   Any teacher who stays in the classroom one minute after the bell is usually in a class by himself.

146.   Then there was the kindergarten youngster who refused to go back to school because it was haunted. After all, hadn't his teacher said that that afternoon they were going to have a talk on "The School Spirit"?

Clothing

147.   One thing about the way youngsters dress today—they don't have to get into their old clothes when they get home from school.

148.   While trying on the suit which his daughter had made for him in sewing class, the father remarked, "The coat fits fine, but the pants are just a little bit tight around my chest."

149.   No matter how we plead to see
                 Our daughter wear a dress,
                 She never puts on anything
                 'Cept jeans that are a mess.
                 And since she will not listen
                 No matter how we beg,
                 We're gonna take each pair of pants
                 And sew up every leg!

Coach

150. The star player on the high school team was about to fail math and would, subsequently, not be allowed to play. The coach managed to talk the math teacher into giving the boy a make-up exam.

"All right," said the math teacher, "how much is six plus four?"

"Ahhh . . . seventeen?" replied the athlete.

"Do you see what I mean?" the math teacher asked.

"Aw, come on," implored the coach, "pass the kid anyhow. After all, he only missed it by two!"

College

151. The two fathers were discussing the seemingly endless college days of their children.

"What's your son going to be when he finishes school?" one asked.

"An octogenarian, I think," said the other.

152. Looking over the bills for tuition, dormitory fees, and books, one father lamented, "If my son gets as much out of college as his college is getting out of me, he'll be a success."

153. "Have you gotten anything out of your son's college education?" asked a friend.

"I sure did," said the boy's father. "His mother doesn't go around bragging about him any more."

154. The dorm may have been co-ed, but the rules were strict.

"If you are found in the room of a member of the opposite sex after curfew," said the dorm monitor, "we will fine you one dollar.

The next time it'll cost you two dollars, and so on until it reaches ten dollars.''

Just then a freshman blurted out, ''If it's all right with you, could I buy a season's ticket now and get it over with?''

155. An insane asylum and a college are alike in so much as they are both mental institutions. They differ in the fact that in order to get out of an asylum, you have to make some progress.

156. One distraught parent claims that his son's college education consists of replacing the three ''R's'' with the three ''C's''—class cuts, co-eds, and cash from home.

157. ''You have to go to college, Son,'' the father pleaded. ''You owe it to your sex.''

''What do you mean, I owe it to my sex?''

''Face it, Son,'' answered the father. ''Those four years are the only vacation a man gets between his mother and his wife.

158. College is very convenient for most parents. It comes at a time when most teenagers are so insufferable you don't want them around the house, anyway.

159. A college education is grammatical—it's a comma, not a period.

Communism

160. During citizenship class the teacher asked Igor why he had defected to America.

''Was the food terrible?'' he asked.

''I couldn't complain,'' said Igor.

''Then the living conditions were poor?''

''I couldn't complain,'' Igor said again.

''Then it must have been lack of opportunity in your job?''

"I couldn't complain."

"Well, then, why did you want to come to America?"

"That's just it," answered Igor. "I couldn't complain—but I wanted to!"

161. Three prisoners in a Russian work camp were talking.

The first asked, "Why are you here?"

His fellow inmates replied, "I was in favor of Bostinovitch. Why are you here?"

Came the reply, "I was against Bostinovitch."

Just then the third prisoner interrupted. "you think that's bad?" he said. "I *am* Bostinovitch!"

162. A Russian schoolboy was asked by his teacher, "What is the size of the Communist Party?"

"About five feet tall," came the reply.

"How did you ever come up with an answer like that?" asked the teacher.

"Well," said the boy, "my father is about five feet ten inches tall, and at least once a day he puts his hand up to his chin and says, 'I've had the Communist Party up to here!' "

163. Two teachers, one American and the other Russian, met at an international education conference.

"I am a subject of Mother Russia," stated the first. "Are you a subject of America?"

"Subject?" said the American. "Heck, no. Why, I own part of it."

Conferences

164. "I think I really did it this time," said the boy.

"Why do you say that?" replied his friend.

"Well, my mother and my teacher are having a conference. I just peeked through the window, and they're *both* crying!"

165. One school administrator met another coming out of a conference.

"Well," he asked, "How did it go? Did you make any decisions?"

"We sure did," answered the other. "We decided to hold another conference!"

Conscience

166. "I have been informed," said the principal, "that you took five dollars to vote for Jones as class president and another five dollars to vote for Smith for class president. Is that true?"

"Yes, Sir."

"Well, which boy did you vote for?"

"Sir!" replied the boy indignantly. "That is a matter between me and my conscience!"

167. Conscience is that small voice within us which tells us not to do something—just after we've done it!

Conventions

168. The two educators were scheduled to debate a controversial issue at the teachers' convention.

"I want you to know," said one teacher, "that the moment we set foot on stage it is going to be a furious battle of wits."

"How brave of you," replied the other, "to start fighting with only half your ammunition."

169. It was the cocktail hour at the last teachers' convention, and a group of male educators was bemoaning the fact that they were dominated by their wives.

"Come on, now," said one teacher, "I want the truth. Every man who does what his wife tells him to do, raise your hand."

All hands went up except for one meek-looking fellow seated by himself in a corner.

"Aha!" exclaimed the teacher. "There's one man who isn't under his wife's thumb. Tell me, sir, why didn't you raise your hand?"

"Well," he murmured, "I didn't really hear the question, but when all those hands went up I remembered that the last thing my wife told me was never to volunteer for anything."

Conversation

170. There's one thing to be said for yawning during a conversation—it is, at least, an honest opinion.

171. Blessed are they who have nothing to say, and who cannot be persuaded to say it.

—James Russell Lowell

172. I don't care how much a man talks, if he only says it in a few words.

—Henry Wheeler Shaw

Cost of Living

173. Nowadays, the only way two can live as cheaply as one is if one is a vegetarian and the other is a nudist on a diet.

174. What we need are stricter labor laws. After all, we have to have something to keep parents of college kids from working themselves to death.

175. The cost of living has risen so much that in Las Vegas, dollars to donuts is considered an even bet.

176. There's one good thing to be said for the rising cost of living: When was the last time you heard of a kid getting sick on a nickel's worth of candy?

177. The rising cost of living changes all types of things. Just think, in a few years a penny-pincher will be called a dollar-pincher.

178. It's getting so nowadays a "wealthy man" may be defined as someone who doesn't know that his son is in college.

179. "Can anyone tell me," asked the teacher, "what the budget of the United States means to them?"

"According to my father," answered one student, "it means that we won't be able to afford a summer vacation again."

180. The price of things has risen so much, that we recently heard a mother saying to her child, "Tommy, you've been fighting again, and just look at that black eye! Come in this instant, and I'll put some baloney on it!"

181. A sure sign of inflation: The woman turned to her nosey neighbor and said, "Who asked you to put your 87 cents in?"

Courage

182. "I really know how to handle my parents," boasted one boy. "Why, just the other day I had a fight with my father, and he came crawling to me on his hands and knees."

"Really?" said his friend. "What did he say?"

"I remember distinctly," replied the boy. "He said, 'You coward! Get out from under that bed!' "

183. When Tommy broke his ankle, the doctor told his parents not to let him climb stairs for six weeks. At the end of that time he was once again examined.

"Good news, Tommy," the doctor said. "You can now climb stairs."

"Hooray!" exclaimed Tommy. "I was gettin' real tired of shimmying up the trellis to my bedroom window!"

184. The father called the boy into his den.

"Son," he said, "I understand that today you stood up to your mother and said 'no.' Well, I'm supposed to punish you, but for that act of courage, suppose you yell every time I hit the desk?"

Courtesy

185. "How do you do?" said the principal to the small student.

"Quite well, thank you," came the courteous reply.

There was a pause, and then the principal asked, "Why don't you ask how I am?"

"Because," the child said, "I really don't care."

186. The teacher called the boy up to his desk.

"Tell me," asked the teacher, "why did you put quotation marks before and after every answer on your test paper?"

"Well, Sir," replied the student, "I figured it was the polite thing to do for the people I copied from."

187. As the teacher took her kindergarten class through the zoo, they came upon a stork.

"That bird, children, is the one which brings the babies to Mommies and Daddies," the teacher said.

Whereupon one tyke leaned over to a friend and said, "I don't care if we are supposed to listen politely, I'm gonna tell her the truth!"

Criticism

188. Children have more need of models than critics.

—Joubert

189.   As a general proposition, colleges are best administered by administrators, next best by faculty, and most worst by students.

—William F. Buckley, Jr.

190.   Humility is not my forte, and whenever I think for any length of time about my own shortcomings, they begin to seem mild, harmless, rather engaging little things, not at all like the glaring defects in other people's character.

—Margaret Halsey

191.   "Mommy, may I please have another piece of cake?"
   "No, dear. It will spoil your dinner."
   "No, it won't, Mommy. Please, just one more piece?"
   "But you've had two already, and . . ."
   "Oh, please, Mommy, please!"
   "Very well, go ahead and take another piece."
   "Thank you, Mommy! And Mommy . . ."
   "Yes."
   "You really must do something about your lack of will power."

192.   The two teachers were heard criticizing that morning's committee meeting.
   "I think it went extremely well," said one, "considering that it was a group of the unfit appointed by the unwilling to do the unnecessary."

Curriculum

193.   We could save a great deal of money in our schools if we only adopted a Core Curriculum. A Core Curriculum is one in which the children bring apples to school. They eat the apples and learn about their nutritional value. This is called *Health*. They take the cores and plant them on the school grounds and watch them grow and flower and fruit. This is *Nature Study*. They sit around under the trees singing 'In The Shade of the Old Apple Tree.' This is *Music*. They are told about Adam and Eve, William Tell, and Johnny Appleseed. This is *History*. They climb up the trees and pick the apples. This is called *Physical Education*. They count the apples and write letters of thanks to the National Apple-Growers Association. These activities are *Math* and *English*. Boys build boxes to store the apples while the girls make pies and turnovers. This is known as *Industrial Arts* and *Home Economics*. They draw pictures of the trees, which is *Art*, and are told how cider is made, which is *Science*.

All these activities have been conducted without textbooks or classrooms and at a minimal cost to the taxpayer.

When the year has been completed, the children eat the leftover apples and plant the cores for the next year's class. Pretty soon, you cannot see the school for the trees—this is called *the end of education*.

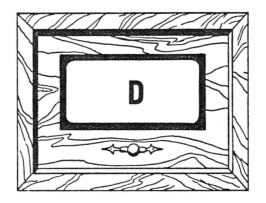

Dances

194. For the occasion of her first prom, the teenage girl was adamant in her desire to wear a strapless evening gown. Her mother felt that she wasn't old enough to wear something so sophisticated. The battle would have raged forever if it weren't for father.

"Let her try it on," he said. "If it stays up, she's old enough to wear it."

Dating

195. At the end of the date, the boy held the girl's hand and whispered, "You are the first girl I have ever loved."

"Just my luck!" sighed the girl. "All I get are beginners!"

196. "Son," said the father, "your mother and I really don't think very highly of the girl you've been dating. Whenever she's here, she sticks her chewing gum under the coffee table, raids the refrigerator, and calls me 'Pops!' "

"Gosh, Dad," replied the son, "I'm sorry, but considering the kind of car you have and the allowance you give me, that's the best I can do!"

197. "Dating is like politics," said one sweet young thing to another.

"Why do you say that?"

"You have to find a fellow who treats you like you're a voter and he's a candidate."

198. Two young men were discussing their romantic entanglements. One lad complained that he was dating a girl who had a twin.

"That must cause problems," said his friend. "How do you tell them apart?"

"I had that trouble," the boy replied, "until I realized that my girl had blond hair and her brother was a brunette."

199. When asked if he'd had a good time dating Siamese twins, the boy replied. "Yes and no."

200. The freshman struck up a conversation with an upper classman.

"I'm really depressed," he said. "I can't seem to find any girls to date."

"Well," said the senior, "I'll tell you my method for getting dates. Go over to the field where the track team practices. You'll find a lot of girls there waiting for their boyfriends who are on the team. Usually there are one or two guys who are late coming out of the locker room. Their girls get impatient waiting and get angry. You strike up a conversation with them, and because they're displeased with their boyfriends, they'll go out with you."

The freshman decided to try it that afternoon, but on his way to the track field, he noticed some very lovely young ladies standing around the football stadium. Anxious to try out his plan, he went no further.

He waited until football practice was over, and sure enough, everything began to work exactly as the senior had told him. Soon, he and a young lady were having dinner.

Suddenly, the door of the restaurant burst open and a burly young man pushed his way to the table and began to berate the young lady. When he had finished, he turned furiously to the freshman.

"And you!" he shouted. "Didn't I tell you distinctly to go to the *track* field?!"

Degrees

201. A B.A. degree indicates that the holder has learned the first two letters of the alphabet—backwards!

202. A college degree does not lessen the length of your ears; it only conceals it.

—*Elbert Hubbard*

203. College life is extremely easygoing. Why, even when the students graduate, they do so by degrees.

204. After he received his Ph.D., the man returned for a visit to his home town in the hills. There he met Mrs. Smedley, one of the town's old timers.

"Doctor, eh?" she questioned. "What kind of doctor are you?"

"I'm a doctor of philosophy."

"Oh, I'm sorry," said Mrs. Smedley.

"Whyever are you sorry?" asked the man.

" 'Cause," she replied, "you ain't never gonna make a living at that. I ain't never heard of anyone catching 'philosophy.' "

205. "I hear your son has a number of degrees."

"That's true. He has a B.A., an M.A., and a Ph.D."

"You must be very pleased."

"You don't know my son; they stand for Basic Ass, More Assininity, and Piled Higher and Deeper!"

Detention

206. "I think there must be something wrong with Billy's teacher," the wife said to her husband. "She's kept Billy after school every day for a whole week. Now, doesn't that tell you something about her?"

"It certainly does," answered the husband. "I didn't know she was a masochist."

207. "Why were you kept after school?"

"I couldn't remember where the Great Lakes were."

"Well, next time be sure you remember where you leave things!"

208. One little boy was complaining to his friend.

"Boy," he said, "I've had to stay after school five times this week."

"Good thing it's Friday, isn't it?"

Diploma

209. A man can get many diplomas in his lifetime, but the one he receives from the School of Hard Knocks isn't a sheepskin, it's a piece of his own.

210. Looking at a professor's diploma-covered wall, the visitor remarked about one which was prominently displayed.

"Professor, is that your Bachelor's diploma there? You know, the one that filled you with so much thirst for knowledge that you went on to start your academic career?''

''Actually,'' said the professor, ''that's my son's birth certificate, and it was his hunger for food that made all those other degrees necessary.''

211. Too many of us fail to realize that a diploma is nothing more than a license to go job hunting.

Diplomacy

212.   Diplomacy is to do and say
             The nastiest things in the nicest way.

—Isaac Goldberg

213. There are three species of creatures who when they seem coming are going, when they seem going they come: Diplomats, women, and crabs.

—John Hay

214. The Diplomat sits in silence, watching the world with his ears.

—Leon Samson

Discipline

215. Many youngsters need to be applauded with just one hand.

216. The principal's name was Barker; and my only clue to his character consisted in overhearing that he was an excellent disciplinarian. I was afraid to ask what that meant, but on reflection concluded it to be a geographical distinction, and, associating him with Mesopotamia or Beloochistan, expected to find him a person of mild manners, who shaved his head, wore a tall hat of dyed sheep's wool, and did a large business in spices with people who visited him on camels in a front yard surrounded by sheds, and having a fountain that played in the middle.

—Fitzhugh Ludlow

217. Most of us will agree that spanking is *stern* punishment.

218. Children can stand vast amounts of sternness. They rather expect to be wrong and are quite used to being punished. It is injustice, inequity and inconsistency that kill them.

—Father Robert Capon

219. A young boy about to be spanked said, "Dad, did Grand Dad spank you when you were little?"

"Yes, Son," said the father.

"And did Grand Dad's father spank him?"

"Yes, he did."

"And did Great-Grand Dad's father spank him, too?"

"He surely did."

"Well, Dad, don't you think it's about time we put an end to this inherited brutality?"

220. The young student approached the teacher with a grave expression on his face.

"Can you tell me if you think it's right for a person to be punished for something he didn't do?" asked the boy.

"Why, of course not," the teacher stated.

"Great!" exclaimed the boy, " 'cause I didn't do my homework!"

221. Ride with an idle whip, ride with an unused heel,
But, once in a way, there *will* come a day
When the colt must be taught to feel
The lash that falls, the curb that galls, and the sting
    of the rowelled steel.

—Rudyard Kipling

222.   "The only position I have for you," said the Superintendent
to the extremely thin young man before him, "is in a class of all but
incorrigible youngsters. Frankly, I think you're a bit light for the
job, but if you want it, it's yours."

The thin young man accepted the position and left. Several
months later the Superintendent wanted to see how he was getting
on, and summoned him to his office.

When the young man appeared, he was smiling happily and
had visibly gained weight.

"Good grief," said the Superintendent, "you must have put on
fifty pounds since I last saw you. Your job must be agreeing with
you."

"It certainly is," said the teacher, "and I don't have any of the
discipline problems you anticipated, either."

"That's phenomenal. How do you control your class?"

"Well, I found out that the only thing they really like to do is
eat, so when one of the kids gets out of hand, I eat his lunch!"

Doctor, The School

223.   The boy was sent to the school doctor with a note from his
teacher which read, "Please do something with this boy; he likes
pancakes."

"Why, this is ridiculous," said the doctor. "I like pancakes
myself."

"You do?" shouted the boy. "Then come with me back to the
classroom. I have my desk stuffed with them!"

224. "I'm not going down there again!" said the second grade boy returning from the annual physical exam.

"Why not?" asked his teacher.

" 'Cause he's not a real doctor!"

"Why do you say that?"

"Because," said the boy, "I put a whole sackful of apples under his chair, and he's still there!"

Driver's Education

225. Three teachers were discussing what was the worst sound in the world.

"It's a moan late at night when you're reading Edgar Alan Poe," said the English teacher.

"No," said the Biology teacher, "it's when you're on a field trip and hear the buzz of a rattlesnake."

"You're both wrong," said the Driver's Ed teacher. "It's the long, low whistle by the auto mechanic who is underneath your car."

226. The young lady was stopped for doing forty miles over the speed limit.

"Miss," said the officer, "I'm going to have to give you a citation for speeding."

"My driving instructor will be so proud!" she exclaimed. "I've only had my license for one day, and already I've gotten an award!"

227. As the motorist drove past, one rainy afternoon, he spied a teenage girl struggling valiantly with a flat tire.

Stopping his car, he got out into the rain and said, "Here, Miss, let me give you a hand."

By the time he had finished, he was soaked through to the skin. As he started to let down the jack, the girl exclaimed, "Please be careful. My Driver's Education teacher is sleeping in the back seat, and I wouldn't want to waken him."

Drop-outs

228. With all the sex education classes in the schools, you'd think there would be less drop-outs.

229. Two mothers were bragging about their sons.
"At least," said one mother, "my son dropped out of a better school than your son!"

230. The trouble with school drop-outs is not that they can't see the handwriting on the wall; it's that they can't read it.

231. Graffiti found on a school lavoratory wall: Don't drop out—stay in school and drive the teachers nuts!

Drugs

232. It is indeed an old-timer who remembers when 'going to pot' meant you were somewhat run-down.

233. Whipping and abuse are like drugs: You have to double the dose as the sensibilities decline.

—Harriet Beecher Stowe

Duties

234. (Someone) said that he was all for education for everyone "anxious and willing to learn." If that were America's only educational duty, we could close down half our schools.

—William F. Buckley, Jr.

235. When the child returned after the first day of school and asked, ''What's sex?'' his mother felt it was her duty to explain, and she began a long and involved explanation of the birds and the bees.

''Gee that's interesting,'' said the little boy as he pulled out his enrollment card, ''but how do I fit all that in this little box?''

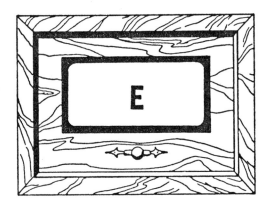

Ecology

236. The crows in assembled convention bemoaned their fate, "The farmers are driving us away from the corn fields. Let us attack. We crows outnumber the farmers. Let the call go out to the crows to wipe out the farmers in a great blow."

"Here, here!" cried one of the crows. "Let the word go out to all. We will destroy the farmers, and then we will have the corn to ourselves."

Then a wise old crow arose, "Hear me, fellow crows. I have lived a long time, and over the years I have observed something which I will tell you. Where there are no farmers, there are no corn fields."

237. While the class was studying ecology, the teacher asked, "Has anyone in here ever done anything in the line of timber conservation?"

"Well," came one answer, "I once shot a beaver."

Economics

238. "Of course two can live as cheaply as one," said a father to a friend. "My wife and I live as cheaply as our daughter at the university."

239. "Remember," said the professor of economics, "running into debt is not bad."

"How can you say that, professor?" asked a student.

"Because it's true. It's running into your creditors that hurts."

240. "Isn't economics wonderful?" said the man. "Take this new car of mine. The motor was made in Germany, the ignition system was made in Japan, and the body was made in Canada. Just think of all those people making a living from this one car—and I haven't even paid for it yet!"

241. When you talk about Federal Aid to Education, let's begin with math. It's about time Washington learned to add two and two and come up with the same answer as the rest of the nation.

242. The teacher was shopping with her small daughter. As they made their way through the crowd, they arrived at the elevators just as the last door closed in their faces and all four elevators started to ascend. The teacher began bemoaning her bad luck.

"Mommy," said the child calmly, "is that what they mean by inflation?"

"What do you mean?"

"Well, everything is going up; there's nothing you can do about it; and you stand around yelling."

—Andrew Dean

243. "Dad," said the boy, "what would you say if I told you that I just saved you eight dollars?"

"I'd say that was fine," the father answered, "but how did you manage that?"

"Well, remember how you said you would give me a dollar for every subject I didn't flunk . . ."

244. The principal of the school threw a huge party for the entire faculty.

"If only my doctor could see me now!" he exclaimed as he ate caviar and drank champagne.

"Why, does he want you on a diet?"

"No, but I paid for this party from the check that should have paid him."

245. The young couple was aghast at the price tags on the so-called 'economy' cars for which they were shopping.

"Why do they cost so much?" asked the wife.

"Well," interrupted the salesman, "did you expect economy to be economical?"

Education

246. Of education, no less than of conversation, the comment holds true which was once made by a southern woman about a dinner party that had failed. "I don't expect anyone to be interested in what I am saying," she drawled, "but I don't see why they can't at least pretend to be interested in what they are saying themselves."

—*John Mason Brown*

247. Very few people can stand the strain of being educated without getting superior over it.

—*Stephen Leacock*

248.   . . . education is largely a matter of indoctrination any way you look at it, and . . . there is no reason to presume unintelligence or shallowness in an "indoctrinator." Socrates was neither unintelligent nor shallow, nor, for that matter was Adam Smith or Lenin. But they did not approach a classroom as a vast hippodrome, where all ideas "start even in the race," where the teacher must interfere with none, because the right idea will automatically come romping home ahead of the others. Their method lay rather in exposing the latent disabilities in all but the winning contestant. "The Socratic Manner," Max Beerbohm reminded us, "is not a game at which two can play."

—William F. Buckley, Jr.

249.   A man only learns in two ways: one is reading and the other is association with smarter people.

—Will Rogers

250.   A real education starts when your father sends you to college, and isn't really complete until you send your son there.

251.   Education is the balance you achieve when you take away all you have forgotten from all you have been taught.

252.   One young man had a highly justifiable complaint after his first day in kindergarten.

"School is silly," he said. "I don't need to be learned to run and play—I know that already. I need to be learned to read and write!"

253.   Education is the technique employed to open minds so that they may go from cocksure ignorance to thoughtful uncertainty.

254.   The man walked into the Las Vegas Casino and placed a wager of five thousand dollars on number twenty-six on the roulette wheel. Twenty-six came up, and the man won a fortune.

As he was being paid off, the Casino manager asked, "Excuse me, sir, but how did you manage to pick twenty-six?"

"Well," said the man, "I had five thousand dollars on me, and today is my fifth wedding anniversary. So, I multiplied five by five and got the winning number."

"But," gulped the manager, "five times five is twenty-five, not twenty-six."

"Good grief!" said the man with fear creeping into his face, "just imagine if I'd had an education!"

255. A man was talking to a group of seven-year-olds about what it was like when he and his friends were young. They had had to walk to school a distance of seven miles each way, every day.

"We all grew up to be successful, responsible men and women. What do you think of that?"

"I think it's kind of surprising," said one child, "since you were all so dumb you kept missing the bus."

256. The janitor had been working at the school for some time, when a member of the Board discovered that the man could neither read nor write.

"I'm sorry," said the Board Member, "but we're going to have to let you go. We can't have someone as a Janitor who can't read or write."

The man left and invested his savings in a small business of his own. He worked at it diligently, and soon it grew and grew. It was not too many years before the man had amassed a small fortune.

One day, his chauffeur-driven limousine passed through the neighborhood of the old school where he had begun. On an impulse, he stopped and went in.

As he entered the office, he was just in time to hear the school board member who had once fired him telling the principal that the principal would not be receiving any new gym equipment due to lack of funds.

The man snapped his fingers. "Write out a check for fifty thousand dollars," he told the chauffeur. Sign my name to it and then give it to me so I can put an X on it."

"I remember you," said the school board member. "You still

can't read or write, but you've become very rich. Just imagine what you would be doing if you had an education!''

"Yes," said the ex-janitor, "I'd still be sweeping up your hallways.''

257. Then there was the child who attended acting school. One night his father said, "Eat your dinner!''

Replied the lad, "But, what's my motivation?''

258. Sign on a teacher's desk: Knowledge is given away here every day. It is free. Please bring your own containers.

Elementary Education

259. The kindergarten teacher is the one who knows how to make the most of the little things in life.

260. Several elementary students were discussing school.

"The worst time in school," said a second grader, "comes at the end of first grade.''

"Why is that the worst time?" asked a friend.

"Because, that's the time you're stuck in school, and you're just old enough to realize it.''

261. "School is a waste," said the kindergarten student.

"Come, now," said his mother, "it can't be that bad.''

"Yes, it is," the boy responded. "There we sit, the whole bunch of us. We can't read or write, and that lady won't even let us talk!''

262. On the first day of school, the teacher walked her students around the building. Finally, they stopped in the lobby before a statue of a resplendant Victorian gentleman.

"That," said the teacher, "is a statue of the man after whom this school is named.''

Wide-eyed, Johnny broke from the group and stood at the statue's base, gazing upward.

"Hello, Mr. Elementary," he said.

English

263.   WHY ENGLISH IS HARD TO LEARN

We'll begin with *box*; the plural is *boxes*,
But the plural of *ox* is *oxen*, not *oxes*.
One fowl is a *goose*, two are called *geese*,
Yet the plural of *moose* is never *meese*.
You may find a lone *mouse* or a nest full of *mice*;
But the plural of *house* is *houses*, not *hice*.
If the plural of *man* is always *men*,
Why shouldn't the plural of *pan* be *pen*?
If I speak of a *foot*, and you show me two *feet*,
And I give you a *book*, would a pair be called *beek*?
If one is a *tooth* and a whole set are *teeth*,
Why shouldn't two *booths* be called *beeth*?
If the singular's *this* and the plural's *these*,
Should the plural of *kiss* be ever called *keese*?
We speak of a *brother* and also of *brethren*,
But though we say *mother*, we never say *methren*.
Then the masculine pronouns are *he*, *his*, and *him*;
But imagine the feminine *she*, *shis*, and *shim*!

264.   After witnessing his parents arguing, the boy was heard to remark to a friend, "Now I know why they call English the 'Mother Tongue.' Fathers never get a chance to use it."

265.   The English Department was referred to in one school as the Chamber of Commas.

266.   "Mr. Jones is the hardest English teacher in school," remarked one lad.

"How hard is he?" asked a friend.

"He's so rough he'll mark off on your paper if you put a period in upside down!"

267.   The overly conscientious English teacher was marking his classes' papers when a student burst into the room.

"Sir," he shouted, "get out of here! This here building is on fire! Them there firemen is all over the place!"

With that, the teacher pulled the boy into a chair beside his desk and stated, "First things first, young man. Now, where did you learn to use demonstrative pronouns that way?"

Examinations

268.   "What is it," questioned the teacher, "that kangeroos have that no other animal has?"

"That's easy," said one child. "They have baby kangeroos!"

269.   The question on the English exam was, "Give examples of the indicative, the subjunctive, the potential, and the exclamatory moods in sentence form."

Answered the student: "I am trying to understand my girl friend. If I understand her, then she will understand me. If she understands me, she may want to get married first. I'm sunk!"

270.   "Remember," said the teacher, "that a fool can ask more questions than a wise man can ever answer."

"Oh," said the student, "so that's why we all failed the midterm!"

271.   During an exam given just before Christmas, the student was unable to answer any of the questions. In desperation he wrote, "God knows the answers, because I don't. Merry Christmas!"

Upon return to school after the holiday, the student received his test paper on which the teacher had written, "God passes; you fail. Happy New Year!"

272. "How do you know I cheated on the exam?" said the student.

"For one thing, your answers are the same as Smith's; your mistakes are the same as Smith's; and, one other thing."

"What's that?"

"When Smith wrote, 'I was absent for this material,' you wrote, 'Me, too!' "

273. "Our teacher is ignorant," proclaimed little Tommy after the first day of school.

"Now, Tommy," his mother said, "it isn't nice to talk that way."

"But it's true, Mom," he continued. "I no sooner got into the place before she wanted to know how much two plus two was!"

274. "Hey, Dad!" exclaimed Johnny. "You know Johnny Jones who lives down the street? Well, he really learned a lesson in school today!"

"Oh, Did the teacher punish him?"

"Nothing like that, Dad," replied Tommy. "He failed every question on the test we were having. Boy, that'll teach him to copy from *me*!"

Excuses

275. At a PTA meeting a mother explained the absence of a teacher by saying, "Mrs. Smith is not with us this evening because every once in a while a wife must give in to the desires of her husband, and tonight is one of those nights!"

276. Mary wore her brand-new dress to the party. Upon her return, Mother was stunned to find that large holes had been cut in the material.

"How did your dress get that way?" asked the mother.

"We played a new game," Mary replied.

"A game? What was it called?"

"Moth," she answered.

277. "And whatever you do," advised the mother, "don't play 'Post Office.' "

When daughter returned, however, her hair was a mess, and her lipstick was smeared.

"I told you not to play 'Post Office!' "

"We didn't," answered the daughter. "We played 'Pony Express.' "

"And what is 'Pony Express?' "

"Well, it's a lot like 'Post Office' only there's a lot more horsing around!"

278. The alumnus returned to his college and couldn't help visiting his old dorm. Knocking at the door of his former room, he was answered by a young man.

Stepping into the room, the alumnus began to comment, "Ah, yes. Different furniture; same room. Different clothes; same closet."

Pushing aside some jackets, the alumnus revealed a lovely young lady.

"That's my sister!" shouted the college boy.

"Different girl; same story," remarked the alumnus.

279. "Johnny, do you believe in life after death?" asked the principal.

"Yes, Sir, I do."

"Well, I'm very happy about that, because while you were absent this morning to attend your grandfather's funeral, he came in here to bring you your lunch."

280. Martin, one of a pair of rather rambunctious twins, was late coming to school one spring day.

"I'm sorry," explained the boy, "but, you see, I was going to go butterfly hunting instead of going to school, but my brother finally convinced me that I should come here."

"That is a good brother," said the teacher.

"Yes, Ma'am. And besides, we only had one net."

281. "Hello," said the voice. "I'm calling to tell you that Mary Jones will not be in school today. She is very sick."

"I see," said the principal. "And who is this calling?"

"It's my mother," said the voice.

Experience

282. Some authorities hold that the young ought not to lie at all. That, of course, is putting it rather stronger than necessary; still, while I cannot go so far as that, I do maintain, and I believe I am right, that the young ought to be temperate in the use of this great art until practice shall give them that great confidence, elegance, and precision which alone can make the accomplishment graceful and profitable.

—*Mark Twain*

283. "I guess my father must have been a pretty mischievous boy," said one youngster.

"Why?" inquired the other.

"Because he knows exactly what questions to ask when he wants to know what I've been doing."

284. There's a saying which goes, "There's no fool like an old fool." Well, everybody knows you can't beat experience.

285. Experience is the child of Thought, and Thought is the child of Action. We cannot learn of men from books.

—*Benjamin Disraeli*

286. "I hear you have a new brother at your house," said the teacher.

"I have a brother," answered the boy, "but I don't know how new he is. From the way he cries, he sounds like he's had plenty of experience."

287. There's a new toy out on the market that requires the child to put square pegs into round holes. He can't do it, of course, but it gives him experience in what he'll be up against in life.

288. Some people's idea of twenty-five years' experience is really only one year's experience repeated twenty-five times.

Expert

289. The visiting professor was introduced as the world's leading expert on guppies. During the course of his lecture, he remarked that he fed his guppies only male mosquitoes.

"But how do you know which mosquitoes are male?" asked a student.

"That's not my department," answered the professor, "I'm only an expert on guppies."

290. An expert is one who knows all the answers provided you ask him the right questions.

291. An expert is one who knows more and more about less and less.

—Nicholas Murray Butler

292. "Remember the story of the blind men who came to study the elephant?" asked the teacher. "One thought it was a rope; another thought it was a wall; a third thought it was a snake. Now, what kind of men were these?"

Answered one student: "Experts?"

293. An expert is somebody who hasn't guessed wrong—yet.

Faculty

294. The two faculty members were known as fine teachers, but they hadn't spoken to each other in five years. Everyone had tried to breach the gap between them; all without success. Finally, the new principal said that he would have a try.

To everyone's amazement, the two teachers were soon talking to each other and seemed on the best of terms.

"How did you do it?" another faculty member asked the principal.

"Simple," he replied. "I told each one a bit of news and made him faithfully promise not to tell the other!"

295. Ms. Jones, a rather well-endowed young teacher, was wearing a gold chain around her neck from which dangled a miniature sailboat.

Mr. Smith, the faculty bachelor, couldn't seem to keep his eyes off it.

"I gather that you really like my sailboat," she stated.

"I hadn't noticed," Mr. Smith replied. "I've been scouting the harbor."

296. The principal, on his routine rounds of the school, stopped in the boy's lavatory, and to his surprise he found the English teacher writing on the wall.

"Mr. Andrews!" he exclaimed. "You! Writing graffiti!"

"But . . . but, you don't understand," Mr. Andrews sputtered. "I was only correcting the spelling!"

Faculty Meetings

297. "Of course," said the principal to the assembled faculty, "you don't have to follow a single suggestion I've made here today—just remember who made them!"

298. After the new principal had addressed the faculty at a meeting, one of the senior teachers came forward and shook his hand.

"Sir," the teacher said, "if you looked out during your talk and saw me sleeping, I must admit that I *did* doze off. But I want you to know that I didn't miss a thing!"

299. The principal came into the Faculty Meeting and lay a massive sheath of papers on the podium, put on his reading glasses, and cleared his throat.

"Members of the Faculty," he read. "Today I would like to tell . . ."

Just then, one of the teachers shouted out, "May I ask a question before you begin?"

"That's a bit unusual," said the principal. "Is the question relevant?"

"Quite relevant."

"Very well," said the principal, gathering the papers of his speech, "go ahead. What is it?"

"Just this," the teacher said. "If you can't remember what you're going to say, how do you expect us to do so?"

Failure

300. They fail, and they alone, who have not striven.

—*Thomas Bailey Aldrich*

301. Failures are the battle scars of those who tried.

302. "I understand that Jones flunked every subject, and the Dean requested that he leave."

"So that's what he meant when he told me that his college had turned out some fine men!"

303. Of all failures, to fail in a witticism is the worst, and the mishap is the more calamitous in a drawn out and detailed joke.

—*Walter Savage Landor*

Family

304. Deciding that his wife needed a little more affection, the teacher bought a dozen roses on his way home from school, and on presenting them to his wife, suggested that they go out for dinner that evening. Immediately the wife burst into tears.

"It's not enough," she sobbed, "that little Johnny breaks my finest vase this morning or that I burn my finger on the iron this afternoon. Now you come home intoxicated. That's all I can take!"

305. From a history test paper: The Bourbons were a French family that used to make whiskey.

306. Why is it that father never believes in heredity until his son gets an "A" on his report card?

307. Then there was the man who was the last child in a family of twelve. He claims that he was seventeen years old before he knew there was more to a piece of meat than gravy.

308. Two teachers struck up a conversation at a convention. Eventually, the talk came around to their families.

"Ah, yes," said one, "I have a fine family of two children."

The other teacher got a far-away gleam in his eye and sniffed back a tear.

"Oh, how I wish I had two children," he said with a quivering voice.

"I'm so sorry you don't have a family," the first educator consoled.

"Are you kidding?" said the second. "I have eight kids at home, but oh, how I wish I had two children!"

309. "Darling," said the principal's wife, "could you walk me out to the curb while I post these letters?"

"Certainly, dear, but why?" replied her husband.

"Well, I want the neighbors to see that you *do so* take me out occasionally."

310. Stressing responsibility, the teacher asked her little ones what kind of chores their mothers ask them to do around the house.

The usual replies of feeding pets, cleaning rooms, and washing faces and hands were forthcoming until one young boy stammered, "Mostly, I just stay out of the way."

311. "I hear you have a little brother at home?" said the teacher.

"Yes," answered the little girl, "but I wish it was a sister. Then we could play house and wear each other's clothes."

"Why don't you just exchange the baby?" teased the teacher.

"Oh, we couldn't do that," said the little girl. "We've used him for a week already."

312. "Dad, do you remember the story you always tell when we go to our family reunion? You know, the one about how you played hookey when you were a kid, and you got caught by the principal and were nearly thrown out of school?"

"Yes," chuckled the father. "I certainly do."

"Well, I guess that just goes to prove the old saying."

"What old saying?"

"History repeats itself."

Fashions

313. Presenting little Johnny with his new brother, mother remarked, "Here he is, and he comes straight from heaven."

Remarked Johnny, "Boy, do they have terrible barbers up there!"

314. "I understand you have a new baby in your house," said the teacher. "Is it a boy or a girl?"

"I don't know," said little Tommy. "Mommy hasn't dressed it yet."

315. "We have a new baby at our house," announced Billy, "and I think it's gonna stay."

"How do you know?"

"Well, he's taken all his clothes off . . ."

Fate

316. The Grand Visir came to the Caliph of Baghdad and implored a favor.

"What is it that you wish?" asked the Caliph. "And why?"

"Oh magnificent Caliph," spoke the Grand Visir, "this morning I was in the market place, and I saw Death. When Death saw me, he raised his hand and beckoned to me. I do not want to die, so I ran away and came to you. If you will give me your swiftest stallion, and if I ride without resting, I can just make it to Samarkand by nightfall. Surely, Death will not be able to find me there.''

The Caliph agreed, and soon the Grand Visir was off riding like the wind to Samarkand.

Then the Caliph grew curious, and he sent his servants to bring Death to the palace.

''Tell me,'' said the Caliph to Death, ''when you saw my Grand Visir this morning, why did you beckon to him?''

''You are wrong,'' replied Death. ''I did not beckon to him. I merely raised my hand in surprise at seeing him here in Baghdad when I have an appointment with him—tonight in Samarkand.''

317.   Two teachers went to the race track one afternoon after school. One man lost consistently, while the other seemed to be winning every race.

''How do you manage to pick winners?'' asked the loser.

''I have no system,'' the other replied. ''Usually, I just stick a pin into the paper without looking.''

''That can't be. Why, you've just had four winners in a row.''

''Oh,'' the winner said, ''I can explain that. You see, after we had lunch in the school cafeteria, I forgot to give back my fork . . .''

Fathers

318.   Said one young lad about his father, ''My Dad can do anything. He can scale the highest and steepest cliff, can swim the swiftest river, and break the roughest bronco. But mostly, he just sits around the house and does what Mommy tells him.''

319.   ''How do you like your hair cut, Billy?''

''I don't!''

''Why not?''

''I wanted one like Daddy. You know, the kind with the big hole in the middle.''

320. Two teachers were discussing their teen-aged sons.

"Is yours one of those 'alienated youths' we hear so much about?"

"I don't know," replied the other. "We haven't spoken in years."

321. A good father is one who can listen to his grown-up son discipline his children and *not say,* "I told you so."

322. Unfortunately, men are generally more careful of the breed of their horses than they are of their children.

—William Penn

323. If I had a thousand sons, the first human principle I would teach them should be, to forswear thin drink and addict themselves to work.

—William Shakespeare

324. Can you imagine what a boy of today will be like as a father of tomorrow?

"Look here," he'll tell his son, "when I was your age I sometimes had to walk *a whole block* to the school bus!"

325. It was the first day of school, and the teacher was helping her small students to fill out their record cards. She would ask the questions and record the answers.

"And what is your father's name?" she asked one little boy.

"Daddy," he answered.

Since this happened frequently, the teacher was ready to clarify.

"I mean," she said, "what name does your Mommy call your Daddy?"

"They don't call each other names," replied the boy. "They're friends."

Fighting

326. Rebellion is in the blood. I cannot go on without a fight.

—Henry Adams

327. If this life is not a real fight, in which something is forever gained for the universe by success, it is then no better than a game of private theatricals from which one may withdraw at will.

—William James

328. "Hey, Willie, I hear you and Tommy almost had a fight today."

"Yeah," said Willie, "and it would have been a good one, only we couldn't find anybody to stop us."

329. There may have been more truth than fiction to the answer found on a history exam. When asked why the U.S. Constitution was adopted, one student wrote, ". . . to secure the domestic hostility."

330. "Mommy!" called one boy. "You'd better come outside quick! Two kids are gonna fight, and you gotta stop them."

"All right," said Mother as she hurried outside, "who are they?"

Answered the boy, "Jimmy and me."

331. When her young son came home with a black eye he had received from a local bully, the mother suggested that maybe he should try to be nice and make friends with the roughneck.

To aid in his attempt, the mother gave the boy some extra cookies and told him to offer to share them.

That afternoon the boy returned home with the other eye blackened.

"What happened this time?" asked his mother.

"Oh, nothing much," replied the son sadly, "he just wants more cookies tomorrow."

332. Sometimes parental logic can be confounded by a child's ingenuity.

Little Jimmy had been getting into a number of fights lately, and his father made him promise that he would not hit anyone again until he had first counted slowly to ten.

Coming out of the house one morning, father was amazed to see little Jimmy sitting on top of a playmate.

"Jimmy!" Father exclaimed. "What did I tell you?"

"I'm counting, Dad," answered Jimmy. "But I want to make sure he's there when I get finished."

333. Because his son reported that he was being picked on by a bully at school, Dad got down the boxing gloves and gave the lad some instructions in self-defense. He also instructed the boy to "stand up" to the bully the next time he was accosted.

The boy burst in that afternoon in a jubilant mood.

"I did it!" he exclaimed. "I did just what you taught me, and I really beat that bully!"

"Good for you, Son."

"Thanks, Dad. Boy, that'll sure teach *her* a lesson."

334.   To fight aloud is very brave,
But gallanter, I know,
Who charge within the bosom
The cavalry of woe.

—Emily Dickinson

Fire Drills

335. Sign on a classroom bulletin board: In the event of fire, simply exit with the same reckless abandon that occurs every afternoon when the dismissal bell rings.

336.   The teacher was very proud of the fact that she had rehearsed her small charges in the proper procedures for a fire drill.

"Suppose there were a fire," she said. "What would you do?"

By rote, each child dutifully repeated the fire drill procedures.

Just then the principal came in and asked to address the class.

"If I told all of you that I'd like to invite you down to the assembly to hear my speech, what would you do?"

In one voice they answered, "We would put away our books and walk calmly out of school until we were 200 feet from the building."

337.   "Did anything happen at school today," asked the boy's mother.

"Yes," he answered. "There was something good and something bad."

"What was the good thing?"

"We had a fire drill."

"And what was the bad thing?"

"It was just a drill; there was no fire."

338.   Teaching fire drills in school is like keeping a family budget. It's tedious, time-consuming work, but the result of poor planning is panic.

Flattery

339.   There is no greater curse to friendship than adulation, fawning, and insincere flattery.

—Cicero

340.   A student was preparing a speech to be presented before the student body. He worked and worked and finally thought that he had it just right. When he had finished, he went to his father and asked him if he would listen to the speech.

"Who, me?" replied the boy's father, feeling rather flattered and pleased.

"Sure, Pop," replied his son. "I figure if you can understand it, anyone can."

341. Deciding to take the newest member of the negotiating team under his wing, the veteran teacher gave this piece of advice before going into the first meeting:

"When you address the Board, don't say, 'None of you knows what the hell you're doing!' That makes enemies. Say rather, 'Only one of you really understands how hard we're all working, and I'd like that person to know that his long hours and gracious consideration is appreciated by all the faculty.' At that point, all the members of the Board will be as receptive as they can be; each one is convinced that you are talking about him."

342. The two co-eds were examining their clothes closets prior to going to dinner with their respective boy friends.

"Oh, Jane, why don't you wear that gorgeous red outfit."

"I really don't think so. It's only for really high-class special occasions," replied Jane.

"Well," stated the other, "maybe you could pretend that Jack was high-class and special?"

343. False flattery and cheap perfume have a lot in common— they both smell.

344. The fly that eats sugar is lost in the sweet and never finds food.

—John Gay

Football

345. Passing through a small town, a man spotted the entrance to a local college. Spying an athletic-looking young man, he stopped his car and shouted, "Say, son, what's the name of the college?"

"Beats me, Mac," came the reply. "I'm here on a football scholarship!"

346. After the football team had lost its twelfth straight game, the coach decided he had to do something to shake up his team. Consequently, he announced that there would be a team meeting to test them on the very basics of the game.

"Now, fellows," he said, holding up a football, "what's this?"

A defensive end called out, "Couldn't we start with an easier question?"

347. The five-year-old really seemed to enjoy his first professional football game. But no one knew how much until the next night at the dinner table when he said, as part of the grace, "God Bless the food, and let's have a big cheer for the cook!"

348. It was the big game and the coach called to his huge left tackle, "Now get in there and get vicious!"

"Sure coach," said the brawny lad. "What's his number?"

349. "What does that new fellow on the team do?" asked the principal of the football coach.

"Oh," answered the coach, "you mean Theodopopopulis? Actually, he doesn't do anything. But he's sure going to drive those out-of-town press boys out of their minds!"

Foreign Languages

350. Then there was the strange request of the first grader who wanted to know if his teacher could teach him the language of Heaven.

"Heaven?" inquired his teacher.

"Yep. My Mommy says my new baby brother is from Heaven, and I can't understand a word he's saying."

351. The foreign-language teacher claimed that in order to speak a language fluently, you had to think in that language.

"You know," said the English teacher, "that's not a bad motto for my class either."

Fraternity

352.   A father thought that he would pay his son a surprise visit at the boy's college. He was delayed in traffic, however, and it was long after midnight when he arrived at the boy's fraternity house.

He had rung the doorbell several times before a pajamaed youth sleepily opened the door and peered out at the man.

"Excuse me," said the father, "but can you tell me if Bill Smith lives here?"

"He sure does," sighed the boy. "Just bring him in and pour him on the sofa. He can sleep it off there."

353.   Three frat brothers were discussing how they had passed their summer vacations.

"I'm glad to be back," said the first. "I swam all day and dated all night. The pace was destroying my health."

"I'm glad to be back," said the second. "I was a camp counselor, and those little kids really did me in."

"I'm glad to be back," said the third. "I worked for my Dad, and I thought I would die from inactivity!"

354.   During a vacation from college, the boy declared that he was going shopping, and his mother asked if she might go along.

At the local department store, the boy began to rummage through a stack of bath towels as he mumbled to himself, "No, that's not big enough; no, that's too small . . ."

Finally, his mother asked, "What are you doing? How big a towel do you need?"

"Well, you see, Mom," replied the youth, "there are forty-five guys in the Frat House . . ."

355.   "Why do you want to borrow my umbrella?" asked the boy.

"Well," returned his fraternity brother, "you wouldn't want me to get our suit wet when I took our girl out in our car, would you?"

Friends

356. He is his own best friend, who takes delight in privacy, but the man of no ability or integrity is his own worst enemy, and is therefore afraid of solitude.

—Aristotle

357. A sincere friend is one who says nasty things to your face instead of saying them behind your back.

358. On the first day of school, the teacher was getting acquainted with her class.

"And what is your name?" she asked one little boy.

"Jimmy," he replied.

"That's fine," said the teacher. "Now, what's your last name?"

"Never mind that," answered the boy. "Since we're friends, it's O.K. if you call me by my first name."

359. "How much is thirty-two minus sixteen?" asked the teacher.

"Sixteen," replied Johnny.

"How do you know?"

"O.K.!" said Johnny, "make it seventeen, then. Let's not argue; I want to stay friends!"

360. A friend is someone who usually has the same friends you have, but always the same enemies.

361. A good-natured woman is all you can expect of a friend's wife.

—Charles Lamb

362. I would not enter on my list of friends,
Though graced with polished manners and fine sense,
Yet wanting sensibility, the man
Who needlessly sets foot upon a worm.
I would choose rather the one who gently passes.

—William Cowper

Generation Gap

363. The best thing about growing older is that sooner or later, you and your children are on the same side of the generation gap.

364. "I remember Will Rogers," stated grandfather.
"You mean Roy Rogers, don't you?" asked father.
"Roy *who*?" said the son.

365. The kindergarten pupil dashed home from class one day and exclaimed, "Guess what! They have a magic record player in school!"
"What kind is it?" his mother inquired.
"Well," he continued excitedly, "you don't have to plug it into the wall. You don't even need electricity or a battery to play it. All you do is wind it up with a crank!"

366. You may consider each generation as a distinct nation, with a right, by the will of its majority, to bind themselves, but no right to bind the succeeding generations, any more than the inhabitants of another country.

—Thomas Jefferson

367. "When I was your age," the father ranted, "I used to walk six miles a day!"

"Yeah," said his son, "we read about those protest marches in our history books."

Genius

368. The boy had received note after note from school. It seems that he always went around with his shirt tail hanging out. Try as she may, his mother could never remedy the situation.

One day she was explaining her difficulty to a neighbor who commented, "I had the same trouble with my son until I did one thing."

"What was that?" Mother asked.

"Simple," she explained, "I merely sewed pink taffeta around the hem."

369. Doing easily what others find difficult is talent, but doing what is impossible for talent is the definition of genius.

—Henri-Frederic Amiel

370. Genius is a crackpot who hits the jackpot.

371. A genius is a fellow who avoids work by getting it right the first time.

372. The man who anticipates his century is always persecuted when living, and then pilfered mercilessly when dead.

—Benjamin Disraeli

373. With the way knowledge has increased over the past few years, the definition of genius is fast becoming any parent who can still help his kids with their homework.

374. There is a sacred horror about everything grand. It is easy to admire mediocrity and hills; but whatever is too lofty, a genius as well as a mountain, seen too near, is appalling.

—Victor Hugo

Geography

375. "Billy," said his teacher, "in what part of the world would we find mangoes?"

"Any place woman goes," answered the wise child.

376. Then there was the social studies teacher who thought he could teach his son about geography through stamp collecting until one day when he asked, "Son, where's Switzerland?"

"That's easy, Pop," replied the boy. "It's the next page after Sweden."

377. A budding sixth-grade economist gave this stunning answer on his geography test: Asked, "In what state is the capitol of the United States?" the youth replied, "Terrible!"

378. "Miss Johnson," said the fourth grader, "how come I got a bad mark on the geography test? I answered all the questions."

"I know, Mark," replied his teacher, "but I hardly think that when asked to identify the Great Plains, I would have answered the 747 and the *Concorde*.''

379.   ''Johnny,'' asked the teacher, ''what's the difference between exports and imports?''

''Well, exports are ports that used to be and imports are new ones that ain't yet.''

The Gifted Child

380.   ''Now, class, who can tell me what letter I am holding?''

One first grader leaned over to his friend and whispered, ''Do you think it would shake her up too much if I asked whether she meant the Phoenician or Celtic alphabet?''

381.   ''Say,'' said one little girl to another, ''do you seriously believe that William Shakespeare *didn't* plagiarize everyone from Plutarch to Bacon to Marlowe? He should be considered exemplary for just his purloining abilities!''

''That may be true, but new research turned up by the British Museum and interpreted by Professor Simon Bartlett of Oxford University would seem to indicate . . .''

''Shhh!'' said the first girl. ''The playground teacher is coming back, and we're supposed to be playing hopscotch!''

382.   One mother reports that the hardest thing about leaving a note for her gifted little daughter is finding it corrected for punctuation, spelling, and penmanship!

383.   The gifted five-year-old was taken to the dentist.

''Now, open wide,'' said the dentist. ''Just imagine that your mouth is the tunnel and this little stick is a train.''

''Certainly, Sir. But I think you'll find that the problem lies in an emplaced lower incisor and possibly a slightly decayed upper right bicuspid.''

384. "Billy," asked the teacher, "how many months have twenty-eight days?"

"Every single one of them," Billy answered proudly.

385. A gifted small girl has explained that pins are a great means of saving life, "by not swallowing them."

—Charles Edward Montague

Girls

386. Mary arrived home and breathlessly announced, "Billy kissed me!"

"Oh?" said her mother. "What made him do that?"

"I'm not sure," the little girl answered. "Maybe it had something to do with the fact that I wouldn't let him up from the ground until he did."

387. "We're gonna be married!" announced five-year-old Susie, dragging her six-year-old intended behind her.

"That's nice, dear," Mother said, "but don't you think you should wait until you've seen a few more boys?"

"Nope! It's gotta be him. He's the only boy on my side of the street, and I'm not allowed to cross over so I can't look for any more!"

388. The girls nowadays display a shocking freedom; but they were partly led into it by the relative laxity of *their* mothers, who, in their turn, gave great anxiety to a still earlier generation.

—Edmund Gosse

389. "Sally, go see if the cake is done," instructed her mother. "Just stick the knife in it, and if it comes out clean, it's fine."

A short time later, Sally's mother was shocked to see Sally repeatedly stabbing the cake with several different knives.

"What are you doing?"

"Gee, Mom, Sally replied, "it got the first knife so clean, it seemed a shame to waste the whole cake for just one knife."

390. One day Mary came home from school and went straight to her room. Soon her mother could hear her sobbing.

"What's the matter, dear?" she asked.

"The kids in school are calling me 'turnpike'!" came the reply.

"Turnpike?" the mother wondered. "Why would they call you that?"

"Because of my figure—no curves in sight!"

Government

391. Federal aid is like giving yourself a transfusion by drawing blood from your right arm, returning it to your left, and spilling eighty percent of it in the process.

392. As the student wrote on his civics exam: "The difference between a King and a President is that a King is the son of his father but a President isn't."

393. And how about this definition from a fifth grader: "A census taker is a man who goes from house to house increasing the population."

394. For everyone was called to consider what a government of nations and empires should be. I therefore say that there are nine cardinal directions to be attended to:

1. The cultivating of each's personal conduct.
2. Honoring worthy men.
3. Cherishing and doing his duty toward his kindred and kin.
4. Showing humble, yet freely given, respect to the high ministers of the state.

5. Identifying, allying, and pledging himself to the interest and welfare of the whole of the body.

6. Showing himself as the father, patron, but not subserviant to, the common people.

7. Encouraging the introduction of all useful arts.

8. Indulgent treatment of men who come from long distances and enter the whole body.

9. Taking interest in the belief that the success of the whole body comes from something greater than a single source.

—Confucius

395. There is nothing to say but that nations spring from THE PEOPLE. For a nation to be free, it is only necessary that she wills it. And conversely, for a nation to be slave, it is only necessary that she wills it.

—John Adams

396. Every man needs a wife, because there are a number of things that can go wrong that one just can't blame on the government.

397. Those who believe in deficit spending should remember that the future we borrow on today will be the yesterdays of our children's tomorrows.

Grades

398. "I may not get the best grades in school, Dad, but you don't get the best salary in your office, so maybe we're even."

399. "Mary," said the teacher, "if you want to get better grades in spelling, you have to pay a little attention to it."

"That's what I am doing," answered the child. "I'm paying as little attention to it as I can."

400. The man's son went off to a progressive college.

"How are your grades, Son?" the father asked one day.

"I'll tell you, Dad," answered the boy. "I'm getting an 'F' in English Literature, an 'F' in World History, and another 'F' in Economics—but I am getting an 'A+' in Sexual Revolution!"

Graduate School

401. Graduate School is a place of transition. Where else can a brilliant young man go off his father's payroll and on to his wife's?

Graduation

402. It was a particularly hot evening in June, and the graduates of Adams College were beginning to squirm uncomfortably as the guest speaker droned on and on.

" 'A' is for Attitude . . ." he began, and he spoke for ten minutes about that virtue.

" 'D' is for Determination . . ." he continued, and this time spoke for sixteen minutes.

This went on until he had spelled out the name of the College.

Rushing outside after the ceremony, one grad pulled off his robes and exclaimed, "Thank the Lord I didn't go to Massachusetts Institute of Technology—I'd never have made it!"

403. Open-air graduations are times when a speaker exhorts the students to weather the storms of life and prays that they don't start during his speech.

404. The teacher was asked by the graduating senior, "Sir, what do you think I should read upon graduation?"

"Well, my boy," replied the professor, "may I suggest you start with the Help Wanted column."

Grammar

405.   I am the King of Rome and above grammar.

—The Emperor Sigismund

406.   The largest preposition-ending sentence has to have been coined by the small child who said to his mother, "Why did you bring that book that I didn't want to be read to out of up for?"

407.   "Honest, Dad," said the boy, "I don't need the talk about the birds and the bees; I study grammar, so I know all about it."

"What does grammar have to do with it?" his father asked.

"Ask anybody who studies it," he replied, "and they'll tell you that only nouns have gender; it's people who have sex."

408.   Then there was the sweet young thing who almost got hysterical when her English professor said that they were going to study syntax in the next lesson.

"Good Grief!" she exclaimed. "I didn't know they taxed *that* too!"

409.   "Can someone give me a sentence with an 'object?' "

Johnny raised his hand and said, " 'I think you are the smartest, nicest, prettiest teacher I ever had."

"Why, thank you, Johnny," replied the teacher, "but can you tell us the object?"

"Sure," Johnny sweetly smiled, "I'd like to get an 'A' in English."

410.   When a thought takes one's breath away, a lesson on grammar seems an impertinence.

—Thomas Wentworth Higginson

Grandparents

411.   A grandparent is someone who can watch a little boy carve his name in the middle of a mahogany dining table with a pair of scissors and remark, "Isn't he wonderful; only four years old and he can spell his name!"

412.   Two elderly women were seated on a cross-country bus.
"You should have seen the funny thing my grandson did at the bus terminal," said one.
"Before you start," said the other, "let me warn you that I have twelve grandchildren of my own, and I'm going to want equal time."

413.   Enjoy your grandparents while they're near,
For some day soon, they'll not be here.
Treat them kind and treat them fair
And praise the God that put them there.
Ever happy and free from care,
Loving, praising—they're very dear.

Guidance

414.   Do not judge a man until you have walked a day in his moccasins.

—American Indian Saying

415.   I cried because I had no shoes, 'til I met a man who had no feet.

—Chinese Proverb

416.   Life is like arithmetic, and love is the only thing you multiply by dividing.

417. "We just got back the results of your aptitude test," said the guidance counselor. "I really don't know how to tell you this, but you'd better look for a job in some field where your father is the boss."

418. Where the blind guides one strains at a gnat and swallows a camel.

—*Matthew, XXIII, 24*

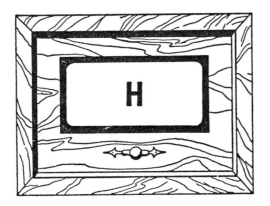

Habits

419. The teacher had just finished her lecture on morality and the importance of forming good and moral habits. Now she was questioning her class.

"What is it," she asked, trying to get the answer 'bad habits,' "that is extremely easy to get into but extremely difficult to get out of?"

One young girl raised her hand.

"My bed on any school day?" she answered.

420. "Mike is a great little boy, Mrs. Smith," said his teacher, "but he seems to have one bad habit. Every time a girl walks by him, he becomes distracted and can't seem to get his mind back on what he is doing. Do you have any suggestions?"

"No," said Mike's mother sadly. "If I did, I would have used them on his father long ago!"

421. Chaos often breeds life, where order breeds but habit.

—*Henry Adams*

422. Ill habits gather by unseen degrees,—
As brooks make rivers, and rivers make seas.

—*John Dryden*

423. Folks ain't got no right to
censuah otha folks about dey habits;
Him dat giv' de squir'ls de bushtails
made de bobtails fu' de rabbits.

—*Paul Laurence Dunbar*

Halls

424. THE TEACHER'S FRIDAY AFTERNOON LAMENT

My students are joyous; the last class is through;
The classroom resounds with their calls,
But I will be happy to get out without
Being trampled to death in the halls.

425. At the end of the school day, a mother was waiting to see the principal about her son. Just then the dismissal bell sounded and a horde of children raced down the hallway and out of the building, nearly knocking the woman over. One last child, however, walked calmly down the hallway and apologized to the woman for the behavior of his classmates. At that moment the principal arrived.

"Please excuse this boy, Madam," said the principal, as he indicated the polite lad. "He's new to our school and is having trouble adjusting."

Health

426. A mother was trying to get her obstreperous first-grade daughter to eat the healthful dinner she had prepared.

"Eat it, Brenda!" she shouted. "Pretend it's the paste in school!"

427.   Methuselah ate what he found on his plate,
And never, as people do now,
Did he note the amount of the calorie count;
He ate it because it was chow.

He wasn't disturbed as at a dinner he sat,
Devouring a roast or a pie,
To think it was lacking in granular fat
Or a couple of vitamins shy.

He cheerfully chewed each species of food,
Unmindful of troubles or fears
Lest his health might be hurt
    by some fancy dessert;
And he lived over nine hundred years!

428. Because of her failing health and the fact that she lived alone, her grandchildren decided to bring a doctor to grandma's home. He gently but firmly poked and prodded, thumped and knocked. After he left, Grandma seemed a bit flustered.

"What was the name of the church that young minister was from?" she asked.

"That was a doctor, Grandma, not a minister."

"Praise the Lord!" said Grandma. "I thought he was gettin' awful personal for a minister."

429. "Johnny," said the teacher, "Why don't you ever wash your face and hands? Why, I can tell just by looking at you that you had oatmeal for breakfast today."

"Sorry, Teacher," replied Johnny, "you're wrong. I had oatmeal for breakfast *yesterday*!"

430. "Mom," said the boy, "I can't see the blackboard in school."

Immediately, the mother bundled her son off to the eye doctor and had him put through a complete vision test.

"Madam," said the doctor after the test, "I find nothing wrong with your son's eyesight."

"You must be mistaken, Doctor," the mother returned. "He told me that he can't even see the blackboard."

Just then little Johnny interrupted.

"Excuse me, Mom," he said, "but I can see it fine once that big girl who sits in front of me moves out of the way."

431. The health of the people is really the foundation upon which all of their happiness and powers as a State depend.

—Benjamin Disraeli

History

432. If we look behind the lives of great men, we find that *history* is often *herstory*.

433. If you study nothing but the battles, you'll soon conclude that the History of Mankind is nothing but a *Scrap* Book.

434. "Johnny," asked the teacher, "what was so unusual about General MacArthur's farewell address?"

"Well, for one thing," said Johnny, "it didn't have a Zip Code . . ."

435. The history class was studying the Revolutionary Battle of Saratoga. The teacher had explained the circumstances leading to the battle and the fact that it was probably lost because General William Howe had remained in Philadelphia and had not proceeded to Saratoga.

The teacher then asked the class to explain in their own words this major British defeat.

One student thought and then said, "Lack of no Howe?"

436. History is a pack of tricks the living play upon the dead.

—Voltaire

437. "Why do we say that Julius Caesar was born in 100 B.C. and died in 44 B.C.?" asked the history teacher.

"Well," answered Billy, "in those days they were all backward."

438. "During the 1960's," the history teacher told his class, "many people protested the war."

"I would have, too," said Tommy.

"Why?" asked the teacher. "Are you against war?"

"I sure am," Tommy answered, " 'cause wars make history, and I hate history!"

439. The history teacher thought that he had done quite a job, until he read one paper which stated, "According to Abraham Lincoln, a horse divided against itself cannot stand."

440. Then there was the history test paper which read, "The Magna Carta provided that no free man should be hanged twice for the same offense."

441. "And where," asked the history teacher, "did George Washington cross the Delaware?"

"At the top of page 178," answered a student.

442. "Suppose you could go back into history and change some things so that they never happened," stated the history teacher. "What would they be?"

The student replied, "Everything on tomorrow's test!"

443. There's one good thing about history, it never has to explain anything. It just gives you the bare facts and then you can't cross-examine them to find out anything more.

—Will Rogers

444. "Mary," asked the history teacher, "can you tell the class what addresses Washington and Lincoln are best remembered for?"

"Sure," answered Mary. "Mount Vernon and Springfield."

Holidays

445. It was her first trip to Hawaii, and the teacher had noticed that several of her fellow passengers did not pronounce the name of the place as she assumed it should be pronounced. Anxious not to offend, she approached the first islander she saw and said, "Excuse me, Sir, but I wonder if you could tell me if it is pronounced 'Hawaii' or 'Havaii'?"

"Havaii," the man answered.

"Thank you so much," said the teacher.

"You're velcome!"

446. There is a vague kind of penitence that holidays awaken the next morning.

—Charles Dickens

447. Wrote the little boy at Christmas time: "Dear Santa, I want a horse for Christmas, but I guess I was good only about half the time—so just bring me a pony!"

448.   If all the year were playing, holidays,
           To sport would be as tedious as to work.

—William Shakespeare

449. "What are you going to leave out for Santa Claus?" the teacher asked.

Various children answered, indicating that they would leave cookies and milk, cocoa, and the like.

"I used to leave that stuff," spoke up little Henry, "but last year my Dad insisted that what Santa would really like was a vodka martini."

Home Economics

450. A mother of a girl taking home economics said to her daughter, "In cooking class do they let you eat what you cook?"

"Let us?" exclaimed the daughter. "They make us!"

451. A woman called up the local bakery.

"You've cheated me," she said. "I sent my little boy for five pounds of cookies, and he only came home with four pounds. What do you say to that?"

"Madam," came the reply, "I'd say you should weigh your son."

452. The Lord sends the food, but the Devil sends the cooks.

—Old Irish Saying

Homework

453. "Johnny," praised the teacher, "usually your homework is poorly done, but this homework is perfect; there's not one mistake. Why is that?"

"Last night my father *didn't* help me."

454. Every night there was an argument in Danny's house, because he wouldn't do his homework.

"Look at Abraham Lincoln," said his father. "He did his homework, and he grew up to be president!"

"Yeah," answered Danny, "and by the time John Kennedy was your age he *was* president!"

455.   To many a child homework is nothing more than skull-drudgery.

456.   "My goodness, Tommy!" exclaimed the teacher. "Where-ever did you get that huge bump on your head?"

"That's where I corrected my father as he was helping me with my homework."

457.   "Your son did not do his homework," said the teacher to the mother.

"I don't understand that," the mother replied. "I told him to do it. I distinctly remember saying, 'Now as soon as the Late Show is over . . .' "

Honesty

458.   And after all, what is a lie? 'Tis but
                  The truth in masquerade.

                                          —*Lord Byron*

459.   In a nationwide poll, college students were asked how they would stop the widespread practice of classroom cheating. More than twenty-five percent across the nation had the same answer. To end cheating on exams, end giving exams.

460.   The question on the job application read, "Have you ever been arrested?"

The applicant printed the word "No" in the space.

The next question was a follow-up to the first. It asked,

"Why?" and was meant to be answered only by those who had answered affirmatively to the previous question.

Not realizing this, the honest applicant printed, "I guess it's because I never got caught."

461. "Billy!" the teacher exclaimed during the test, "I didn't just catch you looking at Mary Ann's test paper, did I?"

"I don't think so, Ma'am," answered Billy. "I waited until you were looking the other way."

462. "Look, Dad!" exclaimed the boy as he held up a brand new twenty-dollar bill, "look what I found in the street!"

"Son, are you sure that you *found* that money? Did somebody really lose it?"

"Sure, Dad. In fact, not one minute after I picked it up and put it in my pocket, a man came by looking for it!"

463. "Class," said the teacher, "you are about to take a test, and I want you to know that I trust you. I trust each and every one of you. That's why I am going to give you this test on the honor system. So if you'll just seat yourselves in every other seat and two arm lengths apart, we'll begin."

464. The star football player was about to be forced off the team because of poor academic grades. In desperation, the coach approached the Dean of the college and swore on his honor that he would give the lad a final exam in his failing subject, and if the boy didn't pass he would take him from the team immediately.

The night before the big game, the coach met with the boy to test him.

"What," asked the coach, "is the name of the first recorded piece of English literature?"

"Coach," replied the boy, "I don't have the slightest idea."

"That's right!" exclaimed the coach. "You don't! O.K., you're in the starting lineup tomorrow!"

465. "I really like this class," said Tommy.

"How nice of you to say that," beamed the teacher. "Why do you like it?"

"Because," the boy replied, "right after you comes lunch!"

466. Honesty is praised and starves.

—Juvenal

467.   Take note, take note, O world!
            To be direct and honest is not safe.

—William Shakespeare

Humor

468. Wit has truth in it; wisecracking is merely calisthenics with words.

—Dorothy Parker

469. True humor springs not more from the head than from the heart; it is not contempt, its essence is love; it issues not in laughter, but in still smiles, which lie far deeper.

—Thomas Carlyle

470.   The value, the worth, and the power of mirth
            Can help each of us to get through
            When the going is rough and incredibly tough,
            And even the sunshine looks blue.
            For once you give in to a chuckle or grin,
            You spirits just natur'ly lift,
            And life is worthwhile each time that you smile,
            For a laugh is a God-given gift.

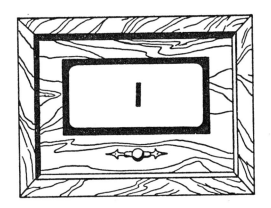

Ideas

471.   I had an idea just the other night;
      A fantastic idea it was, too.
Magnificent, wonderful, clear and concise,
      Ingeniously smart through and through.
It was just unforgettable, wondrously bright,
      Immortal and eternal, too.
And once I remember it, then I just might
      Be able to share it with you.

472. Blessed are they who go around in circles, for they shall be known as Big Wheels!

473. He who sets out to set the world on fire often finds that he has to return home for matches.

474. There is one thing stronger than all the armies in the world; and that is an idea whose time has come.

—*Victor Hugo*

475. To die for an idea is to put a pretty high price upon conjecture.

—*Anatole France*

Ignorance

476. If a person has no education, he just has to use his brains.

477. Everyone is ignorant only on different subjects.

—*Will Rogers*

478. "I read what you gave me," said the creative writing teacher, "and I must say, it was quite prosaic."

"But, Sir," replied the boy, "I tried to write poetry, not prose."

479. "Honey," said the man, "I just can't tell our twins apart. We're going to have to do something so I *can* tell them apart."

"Why don't you use my system?" replied his wife. "I just remember that Little Jimmy has brown hair and little Betty is a blond."

480. "What did you learn in school today?" asked the mother.

"Well," replied the little boy, "in science class I learned that we are bi-peds."

"You tell that teacher she's wrong!" Mother stated. "We are not bi-peds; we're Methodists!"

481. "Dear," said the wife, "Johnny's teacher says that he could use a good encyclopedia."

"You tell that teacher to keep her hands off Johnny," answered father. "If there's any disciplining to be done—I'll do it!"

Industrial Arts

482. The American industrial arts teacher drove to Kennedy Airport to meet his Russian counterpart. As part of a cultural exchange program, the American teacher was to show the Russian industrial arts instructor around the city of New York.

As they drove past one huge office building the Russian asked, "How long it take to put up that building?"

"About eight months," answered the American.

"In Russia, we do in four months," commented the visitor.

A while later, they were driving past a multi-story apartment building when the Russian teacher again asked, "And how long that take to go up?"

"I think it took six months," the American teacher replied.

"In Russia, it take three months!"

At that moment they passed the World Trade Center.

"That's odd," remarked the American industrial arts teacher, "That wasn't here when I drove past this morning."

483. Then there was the industrial arts teacher who was going through the basics with his class.

"This is a hammer," he said. "Are there any questions?"

"Yes," said one boy, "where do you plug it in?"

484. The senior boys in the industrial arts class always pulled an initiation prank on the freshmen. This year one senior pulled aside an underclassman.

"Look," he said, "we just ran out of something very important. I want you to hurry down to the Custodian's supply room and get two quarts of striped paint."

As the boy ran down the hallway, he ran smack into the industrial arts teacher. When asked to explain his haste, the boy told the teacher about the request.

Returning with the freshman boy in tow, the teacher called the senior to him.

"Did you send this boy for two quarts of striped paint?" he asked.

"Y-y-yes Sir," stammered the senior, "I did."

"Well, you should know that two quarts of striped paint are too heavy for him to carry all by himself, so he'll go for your striped paint just as soon as you can find a sky hook for him."

—Dan Sorkowitz

Intelligence

485. "Bobby," said his father, "I thought you said you were going to earn some money by mowing lawns? It's early afternoon, and you haven't gotten started."

"That's why I make so much money, Dad," answered the lad. "I wait until they're half-way through. At that point they're glad to hire me to finish!"

486. Intelligence defies fate. So long as a man can think, he is free.

—Ralph Waldo Emerson

487. When four-year-old Tommy learned to recite the alphabet, his adoring mother took him everywhere and had him show off his newly acquired skill.

One day, after Tommy had gone through the list over ten times, mother chanced to meet an old friend whom she had not seen for some time. Naturally, she told of her son's accomplishment.

"Oh," said the friend to little Tommy, "and what is the first letter of the alphabet?"

" 'A'," said Tommy.

"Isn't that fine? Now, can you tell me what comes after that?"
To which the tired tyke replied, "All the rest of them!"

488. For God's sake give me a young man who has brains enough
to make a fool of himself.

—Robert Louis Stevenson

Introductions

489. We once heard a Superintendent of Schools introduced in
this fashion:
"Ladies and Gentlemen, I'd like to introduce you to Mr.
Smith, our new Superintendent. Mr. Smith began as a teacher and
served in that capacity for five years. Then he became an assistant
principal for four years. After that, he was made principal for
another four years. Then he transferred to our school system and
was principal of the high school for five years. Following that, he
was made an assistant superintendent for two years, and now he has
been appointed Superintendent, and, considering the fact that he's
had trouble holding down a steady job, he's a darn nice guy."

490. The principal was chagrined at the poor turnout at the
P.T.A. meeting. The speaker of the evening had arrived, but there
were less than ten people in the audience. When time came to
introduce the speaker, the principal rose to the occasion.
"This evening," he said, "I'd like to introduce Mr. Jack
Smith, our speaker. Ladies and Gentleman, I give you Mr. Smith,
and Mr. Smith, I'd like you to meet Mr. and Mrs. White, Mr. and
Mrs. Jacobs, that's Mr. Thompson over in the corner . . ."

491. Presently I shall be introduced as "This venerable old gentleman," and then the axe will fall when they raise me to the degree
of "grand old man." What that means on our continent is anyone
with snow-white hair who has kept out of jail 'til eighty.

—Stephen Leacock

492. After he had been introduced by a particularly flowery and praiseful introduction, the speaker rose and stated, "Now I know how the toast feels after the butter and marmalade."

I.Q.

493. A studious scholar named Drew
Took pride in his puffed-up I.Q.,
But it took just one girl
To set him awhirl
When she said, "Drew, high I.Q., too!"

494. Little Johnny came bursting into the house after school one day.

"Mommy, Mommy!" he cried. "Guess what? I know what my I.Q. is!"

"Come, now," mother said. "They don't give out that kind of information in school."

"I know," Johnny answered, "but my records were on the teacher's desk, and I peeked when she wasn't looking."

"Oh," said mother, "well, in that case, what is it?"

"20-20" answered the boy.

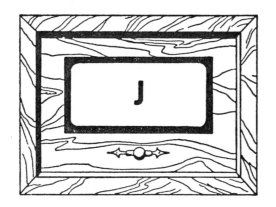

Journalism

495. "Mommy, how come all editors refer to themselves as 'we?'"

"That's easy; Dear," replied Mother. "That's so when the readers don't like what he's saying they'll think there's too many of them to fight."

496. Journalism is literature in a hurry.

—Matthew Arnold

497. A cub reporter on a college newspaper was sent to do the obituary of one of the college professors. He was told to keep it brief and to the point. He turned in this report:

"Professor David Jones looked up an elevator shaft to see if the car was on its way down. It was. Age 62."

498. Journalism consists in buying white paper at two cents a pound and selling it at ten cents a pound.

—Charles A. Dana

499. The editor of the college newspaper called the two fledgling reporters into his office.

"Two lions have escaped from the local zoo. One of them is an old pet, tame as a pussy cat, but the other one is a savage beast—a killer. One of these lions has just been spotted outside the Dean's office, but nobody knows whether it's the tame one or the killer. That's why I want you two to go over there and cover the story."

"O.K., Chief," said one boy, "but why *two* of us?"

"Simply this," the editor replied, "I want one of you to go up to the lion, say 'Nice Kitty,' and scratch him behind his ear—and the other one can write the story, however it turns out!"

500. The editor of the college newspaper decided to try an experiment, and he ran the Ten Commandments in the space where the editorial usually appeared.

The next day, he received a letter from the Dean of the school.

"In the future," it read, "please put some restraint into your editorials. The faculty is complaining that you're butting into their private lives!"

Juvenile Delinquency

501. If his home is happy—if a kid is cared *about,* not merely cared for—he can cope. When I see the "Ten Most Wanted" lists—Wanted posters—I always have this thought: If we'd made them feel wanted earlier, they wouldn't be wanted now.

—Eddie Cantor

502.   Why is it that juvenile delinquency is something that happens to other people's children?

503.   A 'Juvenile Delinquent' may be defined as a 'Child Hood.'

504.   A juvenile delinquent needs a pat on the back—only a little lower!

505.   Juvenile Delinquency is the fault of the Board of Education—it wasn't applied early enough, hard enough, low enough!

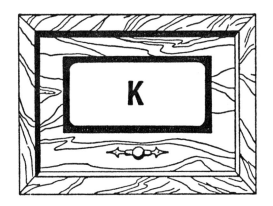

Kindergarten

506. "I think I'm going to have a tough time with this kindergarten class," said the teacher.

"Why do you say that?" asked her husband.

"Well, today was the first day of school, and when I entered the classroom they were singing 'We Shall Overcome.'"

507. In a kindergarten class, several flags were displayed.

"What flag is this?" asked the teacher.

"That's the flag of my country," answered the bright youngster.

"And what's the name of your country?"

"'Tis of Thee," replied the child.

508. "We have a new baby at our house!" little Mary told her kindergarten teacher.

"How lovely," said the teacher. "Why don't I drop by after school and see the baby."

"Maybe you'd better wait until my Mom is better," cautioned the child, "it might be catching."

509. "A bird wears feathers," the kindergarten teacher told her class, "and a sheep wears wool. Now, what kind of clothes does a puppy wear?"

"Oh, you poor lady," little Mary Ellen piped up, "ain't you never seen a dog?!?"

510. "What does your mother do for enjoyment?" asked the kindergarten teacher.

"My mother takes some other ladies in the car," said Jimmy, "and they go to play Bingoawhell."

"What was that they go play?"

"Bingoawhell."

"You mean Bingo, don't you, Jimmy?"

"No, teacher. It's called Bingoawhell, all right. I went with my mother once, and whenever anybody yelled, 'Bingo,' everybody else yells, 'Aw, Hell!' "

511. Mary was having a birthday party and was showing several of her kindergarten classmates through the house. There seemed to be a hushed silence each time a group left the bathroom. Puzzled, her mother listened the next time Mary reached that spot in her tour.

She heard Mary saying, ". . . and this is something you have to be very careful to stay away from. Whenever my mother stands on it, she screams and yells and can't eat anything all day!"

Mary's mother gulped as Mary pointed dramatically to the family scale.

512. "Gee, Dad, I'm gonna like school. It's my first day in kindergarten, and I got an 'A' in arithmetic."

"That's wonderful, Son. How much is one and one?"

"I'm sorry, Dad; we haven't gotten that far yet."

513.   No one welcomes the arrival of spring more ardently than the kindergarten teacher. Not only do her charges get to go out for recess, but she can bid farewell to boots that won't snap, mittens that refuse to fit hands, and snowsuits that won't, can't, and don't zip!

Kindness

514.
A single act of kindness,
Like a stone tossed in a pond,
Sends rings of ripples outward
   That travel far beyond,
And joining other ripples,
   Flow outward to the sea;
A single act of kindness
   Affects Eternity.

515.   "We must all try to be kind," said the teacher. "Especially, we must be kind to animals. Was anyone in here ever kind to an animal?"

Several hands went up, and the teacher called on little Billy to answer.

"And how were you kind to animals, Billy?"

"Once I saw a kid who hit his dog," Billy responded, "so I punched him in the mouth!"

516.   Shall we make a new rule of life from tonight: Always try to be a little kinder than necessary.

—Sir James M. Barrie

Knowledge

517.   He who knows not and knows not that he knows not is a fool, shun him; he who knows not and knows that he knows not is uneducated, teach him; he who knows and knows not that he knows is asleep, awaken him; but—he who knows and knows he knows is wise, follow him.

518.   The true aim of everyone who aspires to be a teacher should be, not to impart his own opinion, but to kindle minds.

—Frederick William Robertson

519.   For he that was only taught by himself had a fool for a master.

—Ben Jonson

520.   "Mommy," asked little Jane, "why does my tummy hurt me sometimes before I have lunch?"

"That's because you're hungry," Mother answered. "Sometimes your stomach hurts when you have nothing in it."

"Then I don't think I'd better go back to school," commented Jane. "I won't learn anything."

"Whyever do you say that?"

" 'Cause," said Jane, "just this morning my teacher said she had a headache!"

521.   Overwork may hurt our backs, but it's disuse that surely cripples our knowledge.

522.   I believe the Lord split knowledge up among His subjects about equal. The so-called ignorant are happy. Maybe they're happy 'cause they knows enough to be happy. The smart one, he knows he knows a lot, and that makes him unhappy 'cause he can't impart it to all of his friends. I guess discontent is in proportion to knowledge. The more you know, the more you realize you don't know.

—Will Rogers

523.   The son of a farmer had come home from his first semester at college. At the dinner table that night he told his father he was studying geometry

"Geometry?"

"Yes, Dad," he answered. "We learn formulas to help us solve problems For instance, πr^2. . . ."

Interrupted his father, "Just a minute, Son, any fool knows pies are not squared; pies are round—it's cornbread are squared!"

524. It is said that desire for knowledge lost us the Eden of the past; but whether that is true or not, it will certainly give us the Eden of the future.

—Robert G. Ingersoll

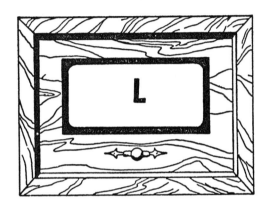

Language

525. "Does your little baby brother cry very much, Emmy Lou?"

"Reckon as how he does a might of cryin'," Emmy Lou responded. "Leastways, he cries whenever he's wet, cold, or hungry. But then, what do you expect—he's way too young to cuss!"

526. Most parents are so happy when Junior says his first words. Big deal! By sixteen he's getting the last ones, too!

527. Rhetoric is language in a full dress suit.

528. Do not talk to me of Archimedes' lever. He was an absent-minded person with a mathematical imagination. Give me the right word and the right accent, and I will move the world.

—Joseph Conrad

529. Without knowing the force of language, it is impossible to know men.

—Confucius

Lavatory

530. The dog show was being held in the local elementary school. The children were overjoyed to have so many animals around, and they were trying their best to be very polite to all the adults who had brought their pets.

One woman who had come to see her neighbor's dog, stopped a young man in the hallway and asked, "I beg your pardon, little boy, but where are the Labradors."

Without hesitation, the lad replied, "It's at the end of the hall, Ma'am—the door marked 'Girls.' "

531. "If any of you have to go to the lavatory," the teacher told the class, "all you have to do is raise your hand."

"I'll raise my hand," commented little George, "but if I have to go the bathroom, I don't think raising my hand is going to help very much."

532. The two teachers were taking a tour of Spain. Everything was going well, until one lady felt it necessary to avail herself of certain lavatory facilities. The problem arose from the fact that neither woman spoke Spanish, while they were in a district where no one spoke English.

The day was saved, however, by the resourcefulness of one woman who asked a waitress, "Where is *la Juanita*?"

533. Cindy and Alice returned from their trip to the lavatory and asked their kindergarten teacher, "What does B-O-Y-S spell?"

"It spells 'Boys,' " replied the teacher.

Whereupon little Cindy exclaimed, "See! We were so in the wrong room!"

Law

534. Isn't it odd that we need a library of law books to interpret and enforce what someone else stated in ten short sentences.

535. The law, in its majestic equality, forbids the rich as well as the poor to sleep under bridges, to beg in the streets, and to steal bread.

—Anatole France

536. When the teacher inadvertently bumped into little Mike, knocking him over in the process, she quickly picked him up and began to brush him off.

"There, there, Mike," she said, "you're all right; you don't have to cry."

"I have no intention of crying," said Mike. "Heck, I'm gonna sue!"

537. Whether mimeographed, hand printed, or just passed by word of mouth, is there a teacher anywhere who is not familiar with:

MURPHY'S LAWS

1. If anything can go wrong—it will.
2. Left to themselves, things usually go from bad to worse.
3. Nature always sides with the hidden flaw.
4. If there is a possibility of several things going wrong, it will

be the one that can do the most damage, or all of them will go wrong.

5. When things are going well, it only seems that way.

538. The interpreters of the laws in Washington can always be depended upon to take a reasonably good law and interpret the common sense all out of it.

—Mark Twain

539. We should be men first, and subjects afterward. It is not desirable to cultivate a respect for the law, so much as for the right.

—Henry David Thoreau

540. We have a criminal jury system which is second to none, and its efficiency is only marred by the difficulty of finding twelve people every day who can't read and don't know anything.

—Mark Twain

Leadership

541. The coach was noted for the fact that his teams never gave up and oftentimes won against superior odds.

When questioned as to the secrets of his leadership ability, the Coach said, "I have no secret power. All I do is try to instill in my boys such singleness of purpose that each one will say, 'If I fall, I shall fall forward.' "

542. The question of who ought to be boss is like asking who ought to sing tenor in a quartet. Obviously, the man who can sing tenor.

—Henry Ford

543. Leadership in teaching is the art of getting someone else to learn something you want him to learn because he wants to learn it.

544. The teacher addressed the class and began, "Class, today we are going to begin a series of lessons which are designed to increase your leadership potential by developing your initiative, your creativity, and your individuality. Now, put a clean sheet of paper on your desk at a forty-five degree angle, and take down precisely what I dictate."

545. The tough little boy went up to a first grade classmate, grabbed him by the shirt and snarled, "Who's the strongest boy in the first grade?"

"Y-y-you are," stammered the victim.

Again the little tough sought out a boy and confronted him with the same question.

"It's you!" came the frightened answer.

Finally, he came up to one youngster and, shoving his fist in the boy's face, said, "Who's the strongest kid in the first grade?"

With this, the would-be victim retaliated, knocking away the offending fist and shoving the attacker to the ground.

"Hey!" shouted the ex-bully, "you don't have to get sore about it just because you don't know the right answer!"

546. There is nothing more difficult to take in hand, more perilous to conduct, or more uncertain in its success, than to take the lead in the introduction of a new order of things.

—Niccolo Machiavelli

Library

547. I have taken a trip on a four-masted ship,
　　And I rode with a witch on a broom;
　　Climbed mountains so high that they clawed at the sky
　　While I sat weaving rugs at a loom;

And of course I crossed swords with some fierce
    pirate lords,
While I whistled a classical tune,
For these journies I took were on pages of books
    That I got from a Library room.
And comic or tragic, a Library's magic
    Can banish all dullness and gloom
And place in your hand the world on command
    And give you the sun and the moon.

548.   He that revels in a well-chosen library has innumerable
dishes and all of admirable flavor.

—William Godwin

549.   The children were being asked what they wanted to be when
they grew up.
    "Anything but a librarian," answered one boy.
    "Now, Tommy," said his teacher, "why do you say that?"
    " 'Cause, the one we have in school has to charge two cents a
day for overdue books, and I don't see how anybody can make a
living on that."

550.   This will never be a civilized country until we spend more
money for books than we do for chewing gum.

—Elbert G. Hubbard

551.   Children's librarians are guided by the principle of appro-
priateness—that is, getting the right book to the right child at the
right time. The librarian was overjoyed, therefore, when Mary Lou
came up to the desk with a book and said, "This is just the right
one. This is just the book I need."
    Beaming, the librarian asked, "And why is that, dear?"
    " 'Cause," Mary Lou answered, "it's just the right size to fit
under the leg of my chair to keep it from wobbling!"

Life

552.   Look to this day,
              For it is the very life of life.
              In its brief course lie all the verities and
                  realities of your existence:
              The glory of action,
              The bliss of growth,
              The splendor of beauty—
              For yesterday is but a dream, and tomorow is
                  only a vision;
              But today well-lived makes every yesterday a dream
                  of happiness and every tomorrow a vision of hope.
              Look well, therefore, to this day.

                                   —Ancient Sanskrit Saying

553.   Every man's life is a fairy tale written by God's Finger.

                                   —Hans Christian Andersen

554.   When the very powerful, very rich man finally died and
went to heaven, he was greeted by an angel who said that he would
escort the man to his heavenly home. After walking a while they
came to a magnificent mansion, several stories tall, and fronted by
marble columns. The rich man began to turn in at the gate.

"Just a moment," said the angel, "this isn't your home. This
belongs to a Mr. Tomkins, who was a teacher who never managed
to save more than a few hundred dollars over his entire life. *That* is
your home."

The rich man looked where the angel pointed and saw a ram-
shackle, small, dusty shed.

"That can't be my house!" exclaimed the rich man. "I was
rich; I was powerful; I was. . . ."

"Sir!" interrupted the angel, "there is no mistake. Mr. Tomkins gets the mansion and you get the shed."

"You can't do this to me!" the other sputtered.

"We have nothing to do with it," the angel said calmly. "Don't you know that here in Heaven we build your home for eternity with the materials you supply from earth?"

555. "All my life is guided by these three words: Stop, Look, and Listen," lamented the married man. "You see, I saw this beautiful girl. I stopped; I looked; and now that I'm married, all that I do is listen!"

556. One life;—a little gleam of Time between two Eternities.

—Thomas Carlyle

557. The professor was troubled by a recurrent dream. Each night he would dream that he was being given the secrets of the universe; the secrets of life. When he awoke, however, he could never remember what those secrets were. This bothered him so much that he went to a colleague and told him about it.

"If I were you," said his friend, "I would keep pencil and paper beside my bed, and try to force myself into waking from the dream and writing down these 'secrets of life' while they were still fresh in my mind."

The professor decided to try it, and that night he did his best to concentrate on awakening as soon as he began to dream.

To his amazement, it worked. In his dream he was given the secrets of life and the universe, and after he had read them he forced himself to awaken. Feverishly he scribbled on the pad beside his bed. When he had finished, the effort proved so much for him that he dropped the pencil and fell into a deep sleep.

The next morning he awoke and immediately reached for the paper. There, he knew, would be the secret of the universe and the secret of life. With trembling hands, he held up the paper and read what he had written.

It said, "Think in other terms."

558. Let us endeavor so to live that when we come to die even the undertaker will be sorry.

—Mark Twain

559. The story is told that a student of St. Thomas Aquinas once found the holy man working with a hoe in the garden of the monastery.

"Sir," the student asked, "if you knew that the Angel of Death would visit you in exactly five minutes, what would you do?"

"If I have lived life as God intended," the saint answered, "then I think I would see if I could finish hoeing this row."

Literature

560. On a literature test, the student wrote, "Shakespeare wrote tragedies, comedies, and errors."

561. Another student answered, "Chaucer was a great English poet who wrote many poems and verses and sometimes wrote literature."

562. Literature is always a good card to play for honors. It makes people think you're educated.

—Arnold Bennett

563. "If William Shakespeare were alive today," asked the teacher, "do you think that people would find him remarkable?"

"I sure do," answered one student. "If he were alive today, he'd be over four hundred years old!"

564. The definition of a colorful story is one in which the main character turns purple with rage, the villain turns green with envy, the heroine's father turns white with anger, the heroine turns red with blushes, and the coachman turns blue with cold.

565. Then there was the man who couldn't understand why his wife was so upset just because they had gone to a Shakespearian play, and he had liked it so much that he stood up and shouted, "Author! Author!"

Logic

566. A teacher wanted to give a rather difficult question in logic one day, so he asked this question: "The United States is bounded on the north by Canada, on the south by the Gulf of Mexico, on the east by the Atlantic Ocean, and on the west by the Pacific Ocean; how old am I?"

After a moment, one of his students held up his hand, and said, "Well, Sir, you're forty-four."

"Why, that's right, but how did you reason it so quickly?"

The student replied, "I have a cousin at home who is twenty-two, and he's only half crazy."

—*James W. Fulbright*

567. The young boy said to his parent, "Daddy, I want to get married."

"Very well, Son," said the father, "whom do you wish to marry?"

"Grandma," the tyke promptly answered.

"Wait a minute! You can't marry my mother."

"Why not?" retorted the little logician. "You married mine, didn't you?"

568. With tears in his eyes, the little boy said to his kindergarten teacher that only one pair of galoshes was left in the cloak room, and that they weren't his.

The teacher searched high and low, but there were no other galoshes to be found. Exhausted, she said to the little boy, "How can you be so sure these galoshes aren't yours?"

"Mine had snow on 'em!"

569. The professor addressed his class in logic.

"By way of introduction," the professor began, "let me begin the course by posing a question. Suppose two men were digging a well. Upon completion, they come out of the hole, and one is clean while the other one is dirty. Which man will go and take a shower?"

Several hands went up, and the professor picked one.

"The dirty one, of course," the student answered.

"Really," said the professor. "Remember, they can only see each other, not themselves."

"I see, now," shouted another student. "The clean one sees the dirty one, assumes that he is dirty, too, and takes the shower."

"I see we have a lot of work ahead of us," said the professor. "How could two men be digging a well, and one of them not get dirty?"

570. "Class," asked the teacher, "which is more important to us, the sun or the moon?"

"The moon," said Ann.

"Can you tell us why?"

"Sure," answered the child, "the moon gives us light at night when we need it, but the sun gives us light only during the day time, when we don't need it!"

571. Thinking is the hardest work there is, which is probably why so few people engage in it.

—Henry Ford

572. Logical consequences are the scarecrows of fools and the beacons of wise men.

—Thomas Henry Huxley

573. "Tommy, can you take your coat off?"

"Sure."

"What about a bear? Can a bear take his coat off?"

"No."

"Why not?"

" 'Cause God never told him where the buttons were."

574. The children were on the playground when the fire engine roared past. The teacher, seizing the opportunity, asked, "Does everyone see that spotted dog on the fire engine? Does anyone know what that dog does?"

"He goes in a burning building and pulls out wounded firemen," said one boy.

"He keeps the crowds from getting too near to the fire," another boy said.

"If he's anything like my dog," a third boy volunteered, "he helps them find the fire hydrant!"

Love

575. The young man said to the girl, "I bet you won't marry me."

Was he ever wrong. Not only did she marry him—she raised him five!

576. "Dear Jane," wrote the kindergarten boy, "I love you, I love you, I love you! Will you love me?"

Came the answer, "No! No! No! No! No! Love and Kisses, Jane."

577. He that falls in love with himself has no rivals.

—Benjamin Franklin

578. Matrimony has its own three R's: Romance, Rice, and Rocks.

579. Isn't it marvelous how before you get married, there is nothing to life but bill and coo, bill and coo, while after you say, 'I do,' it's nothing but bills are due, bills are due.

580. "Suppose I saw a man beating a poor dumb animal, and I stopped him. What virtue would I be showing?" asked the teacher.
   "Brotherly Love?" answered Billy.

581. Everybody loves a lover.

—Ralph Waldo Emerson

582.   The wild hawk to the windswept sky,
   The deer to the wholesome wild
   And the heart of a man to the heart of a maid,
   As it was in the days of old.

—Rudyard Kipling

Lunch

583.   The teacher said, "Class, I've a hunch
   The reason that you, as a bunch,
   Voted my class the best
   Of all of the rest
   Is because it comes right before lunch!"

584. Don't tell us how overindulged some of our children have become. Why, just the other day at lunch in the school cafeteria, we heard one child demand to see the wine list!

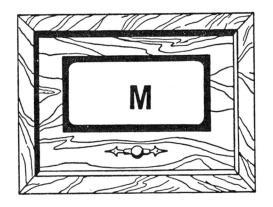

Mankind

585. The child is the father of the man.

—William Wordsworth

586.   There is so much good in the worst of us,
And so much bad in the best of us,
That it hardly becomes any of us,
To talk about the rest of us.

587. Man, in his anxiety to refute evidence that he is a monkey, manages to further the belief that he is an ass.

588. Little monkeys grow up to be big monkeys; little pigs grow up to be big pigs; but Man, wonderful Man, can grow up to be either.

589. There are times when one would like to hang the whole human race, and finish the farce.

—Mark Twain

590. What a piece of work is man! How noble in reason! How infinite in faculties! In form and moving, how express and admirable! In action, how like an angel! In apprehension, how like a god!

—William Shakespeare

591. No voice is wholly lost, that is the voice of many men.

—Aristotle

Manners

592. The elderly retired teacher met the young minister after Sunday services.

"I remember when I had you in class," the retired educator remarked, "and you were just as polite then as you were this morning."

"Excuse me, Ma'am," said the minister, "What do you mean by 'Polite?' "

"Why, your sermon this morning on the various kinds of sinners. I recognized everybody else in the congregation, so it was kind of you to leave me out."

593. "Owww!" howled Johnny in the middle of the Silent Reading period.

"Shhh!" cautioned his teacher. "It isn't polite to interrupt like that."

"I'm sorry," answered Johnny, "but my tongue walked between my teeth and got itself stepped on."

594. The decline in children's manners can be directly traced to the downfall of the woodshed.

595. It was a brutally hot summer's day when Uncle Joe called unexpectedly to say that he and Aunt Betty would be arriving for dinner that evening. All afternoon mother slaved in a furnace-like kitchen to prepare the meal. When they were all finally seated around the dinner table, father asked four-year-old Michael to say grace.

"Dear Lord," he began, "we . . . we . . . I forget, Daddy."

"Come, dear," mother prompted as she smiled at Uncle Joe and Aunt Betty, "say what you've heard me say."

"Oh, now I got it," Michael beamed. "Bless this food, and why in hell Joe and Betty picked the hottest day of the year to barge in, I'll never know."

596. Brenda was told to go to her room because she'd been naughty.

"I'll never send my children to their rooms when I'm a Mommy," she stammered as she climbed the stairs. "I'll just tell them to mind and they will."

Finally she got to the top of the stairs, turned, and loudly proclaimed, "And besides, I'm gonna have better children than you did!"

597. Billy was going to his first birthday party. All afternoon, his mother kept after him about how to act.

"Now, don't hit anybody; don't play rough in the house; for goodness sakes, don't make a pig of yourself at the table!"

Billy finally went to the party, and the birthday-boy's mother noticed that Billy was sitting in a corner watching the other children play.

"Are you feeling ill?" she asked.

"No," he answered sadly, "I'm feeling polite."

598. For dessert, mother brought in a tray with an apple pie and a chocolate cake on it.

"Well, Jimmy," asked father, "pie or cake? Which will it be?"

Jimmy's eyes were wide as he murmured, "Cake."

"Now, Jimmy," father prompted, "let's not forget our manners. 'Cake' what?"

Puzzled, Jimmy looked up and said, "Cake first?"

599. "I hope you were a good little girl in school today," said Janie's mother. "I know how hard it can be to be good when one of the boys smiles at you or tries to make you laugh, but I hope you didn't do it."

"Oh, no, Mama, I didn't. One of the boys tried to make me, but I just went over to him like a little lady and punched him in the mouth!"

Math

600. "Dad, can you help me with this problem? I just can't seem to get it.

" 'If a plumber gets $3.50 an hour and works twelve hours a day, and a carpenter gets $3.00 an hour and works . . .' "

"Hold it, Son," interrupted his father. "Your problem isn't that you don't understand math; it's that you've been learning from a book on Ancient History!"

601. The teacher was trying to impress her students with the use of fractions at home as well as at school, giving such examples as "half a sandwich," and "a quarter of a dollar."

One boy quickly caught on and declared, "My father came home with a fifth last night."

602. One continual activity in match class is the proving of theories. For instance, one student recounted the story of the time he had been traveling with his family in the West, and they had come across three American Indian women, each with her child. One woman sat on the skin of a hippopotamus, holding her baby who weighed twenty pounds. The other two women were seated on buffalo hides and they were holding their babies, each of whom weighed ten pounds. All three babies were boys.

"But what does that prove?" asked the teacher.

"Simple," replied the student. "It proves the old theorum: The son of the squaw on the hippopotamus is equal to the sons of the squaws on both hides!"

603. Answered one student on a math exam: "A polygon with seven sides is called a hooligan."

604. Then there was the student who came up with some unexpected insight when he answered, "Algebraic symbols are used when you don't know what you are talking about."

605. "I think our teacher is crazy," said Tommy as he walked in from school.

"Why do you say that?" asked his mother.

"Well, yesterday she told us that five plus five equaled ten. That's O.K., but today she said it could be seven plus three, six plus four, eight plus two, or nine plus one! If she can't make up her mind, how am I supposed to?"

606. "Daddy," the child asked, "how do you find the least common denominator?"

"Good grief!" exclaimed father. "You mean they haven't found that yet?!?"

607. Then there was the student who added the column of figures ten times and couldn't understand why his math professor was upset with him when he asked what should be done with the ten answers he had gotten.

Medicine

608. Little Billy came from a large family. Periodically throughout his ten years, his mother had gone to the hospital and returned with a baby brother or sister.

One day his father fell from a ladder, broke his leg, and was taken to the hospital to have it set.

During visiting hours, Billy tiptoed into the room, showed his father both sides of his clean hands, and said, "I been good, Daddy, and my hands are clean—Can I hold the baby now?"

609. It was time for the first-graders to have their first school physical. Their teacher was telling them how to address the doctor.

"You may say, 'Good morning, Doctor' or 'Hello, Sir.' "

Matthew couldn't seem to get it right. In desperation, the teacher finally said, "Just say what your father says when he goes to the doctor."

Imagine her embarrassment when little Matt met the doctor and piped up with, "And how much is *this* going to cost?"

610. A young college student was out on a date with a not-too-bright young lady.

"What are you taking in college?" she asked

"Medicine," came his proud reply.

"Well, I sure hope what you've got isn't catching, and you get over it soon."

611. The medical student hasn't been seen in any of the college haunts for some time. Then one night he appeared at his favorite spirit spot, started buying drinks for everyone, and seemed happier than ever.

"Welcome back," said the bartender. "What happened to you? Where were you?"

"Boy, it's been rough. We've been going through the various medical rotations. Each time we studied something, I swore *I* had it.

So far I've had gall stones, heart attacks, gambling paranoia, and just last week I thought my hair was falling out. But now I can relax—today we moved into obstetrics!''

612. One doctor was known for his reluctance to make house calls. Late one night he received a phone call from a distraught lady.

"My grandfather thinks he's sick. Will you come to see him?"

"I saw him only last week," the doctor replied, "and he seemed fine."

He hung up and thought no more about it until he saw the woman on the street about a week later.

"How's your grandfather?" he inquired. "Does he still think he's sick?"

"No," she answered, "now he thinks he's dead."

Memory

613.
   I can't sing the old songs now!
    It's not that I deem them low;
   'Tis that I can't remember how
    They go.

       —Charles Stuart Calverley

614. Two anthropology professors were arguing that each had found the world's greatest memory expert.

"I know of an old Indian," said one, "who was absolutely phenomenal. Let's see, I haven't seen him for fifteen years, but I was looking at my journals the other night, and I recorded that the last thing we were talking about was how he liked his eggs cooked."

"He can't be so extraordinary in memory," said the other. "Let's go find him."

The two men searched for several months. Finally, they approached the old Indian's village.

The first professor raised his hand in the traditional Indian greeting.

"How," he called.

The Indian looked up and said, "Scrambled."

615. As I grow older, I find that I have trouble remembering three things—the first is names, the second is telephone numbers, and the third . . . the third . . . er . . . the third . . .

616. The young man went up to the druggist.

"I'd like some $C_9H_8O_4$, that's acetylsalicylic acid in crystalline form," he said.

"Do you mean aspirin?" asked the druggist.

"That's it. You know, I can never remember that name."

617. "Professor," said the student, "I was working in the library, and I came across this paper that you wrote about twenty-five years ago. I wonder if you could explain it to me."

The professor reviewed what he had written. Finally, he lowered the text and addressed the student.

"Son," he said, "I must apologize. When I wrote that paper twenty-five years ago, the meaning was known but to me and God. Now, I'm afraid only God remembers."

618. "Boy, am I worried," said one teacher. "I'm really losing my memory, and I don't know what to do about it."

Counselled his colleague, "Forget it."

Men and Women

619. In the battle of the sexes one is either a man or a woman— you can't be neutral!

620. There're few things truer than the statement that the only time a woman changes a man is when he's a baby.

621. "I never take my troubles home with me from school," said one teacher.

"Me neither," said his friend. "Mine's there waiting for me!"

622. "Football! Football! Football!" shouted the wife as her husband sat glued to the T.V. "I think I'd drop dead if you spent a Sunday afternoon talking to me."

"It's no use," mumbled her husband, "you can't bribe me."

623. "Morality and the stereotyping of sex roles are changing so rapidly that I predict that in the near future women will be proposing to men," said the Social Psychologist during his lecture.

"Big deal," whispered one member of the audience to another. "It'll probably be the time *he* discovers that fish swim and birds fly."

624. To most mothers, Women's Liberation means the first day school is in session.

625. Questioned the teacher, "What is the chief cause of divorce?"

Answered the student, "Marriage."

626. The husband looked adoringly at his wife and whispered, "Didn't I tell you that I would see us over the rough spots in life?"

"You certainly did, dear," his wife replied, "and you haven't missed a single one of them."

627. Wrote the student: "In Christianity, a man can only have one wife. This is called monotony."

628. "Dear," said the husband, "I'm going to invite our daughter's boy friend over for dinner tonight."

"What!" exclaimed the wife. "The place is a mess, the baby has colic, all we have in the refrigerator are leftovers, the toilet is backed up and must be fixed at once, and you want to invite Betty's boyfriend for dinner. You must be out of your mind!''

"Not at all,'' answered the husband. "I think our daughter is far too young to get married, and I don't want that young man of her's getting any ideas.''

629.   A system could not well have been devised more studiously hostile to human happiness than marriage.

—Percy Bysshe Shelley

Mental Health

630.   It is a proven fact that insanity is hereditary—parents get it from their children.

631.   The boy was rather small, and he'd been used to sleeping with a night light on. After much discussion, his parents had decided it was time for him to sleep in the dark.

"Must I sleep in the dark?'' the boy asked the first night the light went off.

"You're a big boy now, darling,'' his mother explained. "Besides, there isn't anything in the dark that could hurt you.''

"In that case,'' said the boy, "I'd like to get up and say my prayers more carefully—just for my own peace of mind!''

632.   After Mr. Jones suffered a nervous breakdown he committed himself to a local sanitorium for rest and recuperation.

One day, the attending doctor saw Mr. Jones on the grounds.

"You've shown tremendous improvement,'' the doctor said. "We are going to release you in two weeks. Why don't you write to your family that they can pick you up at that time?''

Joyfully, Mr. Jones wrote the letter. When he finished and sealed it, he was licking the stamp when it slipped through his fingers, fell to the floor, and stuck to the back of a cockroach that was passing by. Mr. Jones had not seen the cockroach. What he did see, however, was his escaping stamp zig-zaging across the floor, going over the baseboard, slowly ambling up the wall, across the ceiling, and finally heading toward a crack on the other wall and disappearing.

With a long, depressed sigh he tore up the letter.

"Two weeks, hell," he said. "I won't be ready to leave for two *years*!"

Military

633. A young army recruit named Frank
Said, "There's two things on which you can bank:
I don't like to work,
And I'm kind of a jerk—
So I'm bound to make General's rank!"

634. Ask any of the soldiers in boot camp, and they'll tell you that Army Intelligence is a contradiction in terms.

635. The Sergeant lined up the recruits.

"Men," he bellowed, "the Captain wants me to tell you guys that as part of the Army's cultural program you are going to be marched over to the base lecture hall where you're going to be given a lecture on Keats. I want you guys to listen carefully, and I want you to ask intelligent questions."

With that he leaned in to the nearest recruit.

"And you," he whispered, "make sure you ask him what a 'Keat' is."

Misfortune

636. "What is it?" asked the woman when her friend showed up in tears. "What happened?"

"It's my husband," she sobbed. "He's left home!"

"There, there," the friend consoled, "he's left home before, and he's always returned."

"But this time it's for good," the other wailed. "He took his golf clubs!"

637.   Mishaps are like knives, that either serve us or cut us, as we grasp them by the blade or the handle.

—James Russell Lowell

638.   The little girl came sobbing to her mother.

"Tommy's mean," she said of her brother. "He just broke my favorite doll!"

"Oh, darling," said Mother, "I'm sure he didn't mean it. How did it happen?"

"He did so!" answered the little girl. "He was eating a jelly sandwich, and I asked him for a bite. He wouldn't let me, so I smashed him over the head with my doll!"

639.   Socrates thought that if all our misfortunes were laid in a common heap, where everyone would have to take an equal part, most people would be contented to take their own and depart.

—Plutarch

640.   The worst is not if we can say, "This is the worst."

—William Shakespeare

Mistakes

641.   Even the youngest of us may be wrong sometimes.

—George Bernard Shaw

642.   The nursery school teacher was trying to get American history across on a very basic level.

"When we say, 'Declaration of Independence,' " she told her class, "what we really mean is that some people got together and wrote a letter which said that everybody in America is free."

"That's not true," yelled one voice. "Everybody in America is not free—I'm four!"

643.   Experience is the name that everyone gives to his mistakes.

—Oscar Wilde

644.   The teacher was driving down the highway when she was stopped by a policeman who asked to see her driver's license. It turned out to be a restricted one which required the woman to wear glasses while driving.

"I thought you had trouble seeing," remarked the officer. "I'm afraid I'm going to have to give you a summons."

"Officer," said the woman, "you don't understand. I have contacts."

"I don't care who you know!" exclaimed the policeman. "You're getting a ticket!"

645.   "I don't think Mr. Jones likes Mrs. Jones," said little Jimmy.

"Come, now, Jimmy," his mother admonished, "how can you say that, Why, Mrs. Jones just had a lovely little baby girl, and I know they're both overjoyed."

"I don't think so. This afternoon I was passing Mr. Jones' grocery store, and I saw him put a sign in the window which said, 'Boy Wanted.' "

Misunderstanding

646.   Because half-a-dozen grasshoppers under a fern make the field sing with their importunate chink, whilst thousands of great cattle, reposed beneath the shadow of the British Oak, chew the cud and are silent, pray do not imagine that those who make the noise are the only inhabitants of the fields; that of course they are many in number; or that, after all, they are other than the little shriveled meager, hopping, the loud and troublesome insects of the hour.

—Edmund Burke

647. "Mommy! Mommy! Jimmy's gonna do a bad thing!" gushed little five-year-old Betsy.

"Calm down, dear," said Mother. "What's this about your brother doing something wrong?"

"Well, you told us never to steal, and I just heard Jimmy tell his friend that he was gonna hold up the bride's train during the wedding on Saturday."

648. The local sheriff and his deputy were driving down a twisting country lane when they were passed by two long-haired types on motorcycles going the other way.

"Pigs!" the cyclists screamed in passing.

"Hippy freaks!" yelled back the sheriff.

Then the sheriff took a curve in the road and almost plowed headlong into the largest herd of pigs he'd ever seen.

649. Then there was the politician who was stirring up the local townspeople against his opponent.

"My opponent is a hopeless extrovert, a confirmed carnivore, and besides, his sister is a thespian in New York!"

650. "Is this letter for you?" inquired the new mailman. "See, the name is illegible."

"Sorry Son, but I guess not," said the old codger. "My name is Bill Jones."

651. "I don't think our teacher is ever going to go on another vacation with her new husband after the terrible time they must have had on their honeymoon," reported eight-year-old Wendy.

"Why do you say that?" asked her mother.

"Well, she *said* it was fun, but I could tell it wasn't. They went all the way to Hawaii, but she doesn't talk about what they did, and she didn't even get a sun tan!"

Money

652. If you want to know what God thinks of money, just look at the people He's giving it to.

—New England Proverb

653. Two teachers met in their local Credit Union. They soon discovered that both were there to take out a loan.

"I'm here because of my wife," said the first, "and her strict bill-paying philosophy."

"But," answered the other, "I see your wife out shopping, and she always seems to have money to spend."

"That's what I meant about paying bills. She never pays old bills, and those that are new she lets slide until they're old!"

654. "Class," said the home economics teacher, "for the next two weeks I want you to keep a journal of every product that you buy."

At the end of the two week period, the teacher again addressed the class.

"Well," she said, "and what did you learn from keeping the journal? Sally?"

"Ma'am," answered Sally, "I learned not to buy anything I couldn't spell."

655. The rush was on for after-school jobs around town. The local grocer, for example, was beseiged by responses to his "Help Wanted" sign. The lad who finally got the job was awarded the position for honesty. In the space marked, "Salary Desired" the boy had written, "Of course, how else could I afford to date?"

656. "Mommy," said little Bess, "how much am I worth to you?"

"Why, you're worth a million dollars to Daddy and me," replied the mother.

"In that case," Bess stated, "could you advance me fifty cents?"

657. If you think that kids are not aware of math and money, just try borrowing from them and watch the compound interest rise.

658. A gunman held up the payroll office of a local school district.

"Never mind the salaries," he demanded, "just give me the dues, tax, and pension deductions."

659. Daddy's little girl came home on semester break and announced that she had decided on her life's career.

"My English professor says I have a definite talent," she said. "He claims I can write for money."

"I agree," said her father. "In fact, that's all you've done since you left for college."

660.   You must leave your many millions
                   And the gay and festive crowd;
                   'Though you roll in royal billions,
                   There's no pocket in a shroud.

                                   —*John Alexander Joyce*

Mothers

661. The mother's heart is called the child's schoolroom.

                                   —*Henry Ward Beecher*

662. Any mother will tell you that there is only one truly beautiful child in this world—and she has it.

663. The teacher gave her third-graders a lesson on magnetism and its properties. After the lesson, she began to ask questions.

"My name starts with an 'M,' " she told one little boy, "and I pick up things. What am I?"

"Without hesitation, the lad replied, "A mother."

664. Johnny came into the living room and announced to his parents that he had a problem. It seemed that the next day was his girl's birthday, and he couldn't think of anything to get her.

"Mother," he asked, "if you were sixteen tomorrow, what would you want?"

With a wistful look his mother replied, "Not another blessed thing!"

665. When the boy arrived at camp, he followed his counselor to the cabin and began to unpack.

"What's all this?" asked the counselor as he pointed to a pair of galoshes, a can of disinfectant spray, and a hot water bottle. "You're only going to be staying for two weeks."

"Sir," said the lad with a sigh, "didn't you ever have a mother?"

666. God can't be always everywhere: and, so,
Invented Mothers.

—Sir Edwin Arnold

667. Then there was the boy whose family was so large that he thought that 'Obstetrics' was a disease his mother caught once every year.

Movies

668. There's only one thing that can kill the Movies, and that's education.

—Will Rogers

669.   It is not true that kids will watch anything on the movie screen. Why just the other day, there was a boy who told his parents that the movie he had seen with his girl friend was so bad, they had to force themselves to sit through it the sixth and seventh times.

670.   I wish I hadn't broke that dish,
                     I wish I was a movie-star,
                     I wish a lot of things, I wish
                     That life was like the movies are.

                                        —*Sir Alan Patrick Herbert*

671.   When the young boy showed up at the local movie theater for a matinee on a school day, the manager took him aside.

"Now, look, Son," the man said as he put his arm around the boy, "I can understand how a lad your age might want to play hookey, but . . ."

At this point the youth interrupted the manager and motioned him to come closer. The man leaned down to the boy.

"I ain't playing hookey," the boy whispered, "I really do have the flu!"

Music

672.   There are many, many people in this country who can neither read nor write, yet make a good living. They write rock and roll songs.

673.   Mother decided that it was about time there was some music in the house, so she went out and bought a piano. On the day it arrived, little Mark banged and banged and banged on the keyboard, and ran, at last to his mother.

"Mommy," he cried, "you got a stupid piano. It don't know any of the songs I know!"

674.   Well into their vacation, the family found that they had left all clocks and watches at home. That would not have been so bad except for the fact that mother had to know the exact time in order to give baby her medicine. The motel at which they were staying did not have desk service nor was there a television or radio in the room. They were at a loss to know the correct time until Junior came up with an idea.

He merely took out his clarinet and began to play. Sure enough, not a minute later a voice yelled out, ''Cut out that music; don't you know it's one in the morning!?!''

675. Because he was the music teacher at the local elementary school, Mr. Edwards was always being asked to listen to see if little Mary or Judy or Barbara had any real talent.

One afternoon he was again subjected to an excruciating rendition of *Clair de Lune*. As ever, he smiled and nodded.

The doting mother leaned over and said, ''I'm so glad you like good music.''

''Indeed I do, Madam,'' he replied, ''but your child can keep on playing anyhow.''

676. How far has music gone today? Well, at a local junior high school dance, someone set off the fire alarm and ten couples got up and danced.

677. Musical training is a more potent instrument than any other, because rhythm and harmony find their way into the inward places of the soul.

—Plato

Music Instruction

678. After only two year's instruction in music, little Alfred wrote on a test, ''S.O.S. is the musical term meaning 'Same Only Softer.' ''

679. A music teacher is a bridge-builder. He tries to span the gap between his student's hands and the melodies of the Masters.

680. When you've just bought a brand new piano, that is the moment when what you don't want is an honest opinion from your son's music teacher.

681. "I never have any behavioral problems in my music classes," said the music teacher.

"What's your secret?" asked a friend.

"Simple. I inform them that if they misbehave, I'll tell their parents that they have talent."

Music Recitals

682. The school newspaper sent a reporter to cover the annual band concert. The story he wrote was to the point.

"Last night," it stated, "our band played Handel. Handel lost."

683. "I'm never going to be an opera singer," said little Beth after her first opera, "it hurts too much."

"But, dear," mother asked, "it doesn't hurt to sing."

"Oh, yeah," Beth returned, "then why was the lady screaming like that?"

684. It was reported that Leopold Stokowsky, the late and great conductor, once told a noisy audience, "A painter paints his pictures on canvas. Musicians paint their pictures on silence. We provide the music, and you provide the silence."

685. Instead of watching the Sunday afternoon football game, the teacher's wife, an opera buff, dragged him to a performance of *Aida*. Noticing that the conductor always looked at a book before him, the teacher whispered, "What's that volume to which he keeps referring?"

"That's the score, dear."

"Really," he said as his eyes brightened, "who's winning?"

686.   Little Peter was taken to the opera for the first time. Prior to his visit, he was carefully rehearsed as to his behavior. He was not to fidget, yawn, make noise, or move about too much, and, indeed, he was a perfect little gentleman all through the performance.

"You've been very good, Peter," said his mother as the final curtain descended. "As a reward, you can do whatever you like."

Peter screamed.

687.   It was a tradition that on the Prince's twelfth birthday his father, the King, would take him to his first opera.

The performance was interminably long and the songs were sung with great fervor because of the royal presence.

At last it was over, and the exhausted Prince questioned his father as to the necessity of such a tradition.

"Well, my Son," the old man said, "wearing the crown sometimes leads men to do deeds which are against all laws. Those poor devils are stripped of their royal privileges and cast into prisons."

"I understand, Father, but why the opera?"

"These same players whom you saw tonight, also perform in our prisons. It will help you to do right when you are tempted, if you will remember that fact."

688.   The music teacher held a recital for her students and their families. All seemed to go well, and after the concert, cake and ice cream were served.

The teacher noticed the small brother of one of her students enjoying a heaped plate of goodies.

"Well, Tommy," she asked, "I trust you enjoyed the concert?"

"Oh, yes, Ma'am," little Tommy replied, "everything except the music."

689.   The little girl sang while her brother accompanied her on the piano. After the recital, he ran up to his mother and yelled, "It wasn't my fault! It didn't matter if I played on the white keys or the black keys—*she* kept singing in the cracks!"

Nature Study

690. After showing her students several slides of creatures in their wild habitat, the teacher asked, "Where are elephants found?"

An amazed little boy answered, "Gee, Miss Wilson, they're so big, how could they ever get lost?"

691. "Our teacher told us that some birds eat fruit," said Mike, "but I don't believe her."

"Why not?" asked his brother.

"I can't see how they could open the cans."

692. I guess it's too late for Mankind to either go back to order in Nature or truth in history.

—John R. Paxton

693. "Nature sure is a fantastic planner, isn't she?" said Bobby to his teacher.

"How so, Bobby?"

" 'Cause, she plans for things even before they happen."

"Could you give me an example of what you mean?" asked the teacher.

"Sure," answered Bobby, "just look at where she put our ears. They're just right for holding up eyeglasses."

694.   There is pleasure in the pathless woods,
There is rapture on the lonely shore,
There is society, where none intrudes,
By the deep sea, and music in it's roar:
I love not man the less, but Nature more.

                        —*Lord Byron*

Notes

695. "I don't mind that child being absent," the teacher told her colleague. "In fact, the way he behaves in class, his parents should be required to write a note explaining his presence!"

696. A business teacher uses this story to show the value of effective personal relations:

Going through the first-of-the-month bills, Mr. Thomas was shocked to find in one of them the note, "SECOND NOTICE—PLEASE PAY PROMPTLY TO AVOID LITIGATION."

He immediately called the company to apologize and to promise immediate payment. He couldn't help but remark, in his own behalf, that he hadn't received any prior notice.

"Oh, don't let that bother you, Mr. Thomas," said the credit manager. "We started enclosing that note in all our billing. You'd be surprised how effective it's been."

697. One of the cleverest notes from school has to have come from the second grade teacher who wrote: "To All Parents—I promise not to believe everything your children say about you if you promise not to believe everything they say about me."

698. "Gosh, teachers are smart," said Stanley as he gave his mother a note from his teacher.

His mother read the note detailing his progress and then noticed a postscript underlined in red. It started: "Dear Stan—Now that you've read this, be sure to give it to your mother."

699. Taped to the refrigerator door: "Mommy, I am roller skating with Johnny. I will be home in time for dinner. Love, Bobby— P.S. When is dinner?"

700. "What are you doing?" asked the father when he found his wife sniffling at the table.

"I suppose this is the last thing I'll be putting in Johnny's Baby Book," she sighed sentimentally. "It's a note from his teacher asking why we ever had him."

Nurse, The School

701. After being given his flu shot at school, Billy looked concerned as the Nurse started to place a band-aid over the injection spot.

"This is nothing to worry about," she said. "It just shows where you've had a needle. Besides, we don't want any of your friends to accidentally hit you on your sore arm, do we?"

"No, Ma'am," Billy replied, "but could you please put it on my other arm. You don't know my friends!"

702. The Nurse conducted the class in Health, but she wasn't quite prepared for the answers she received to the question asking for the qualifications of a good nurse.

"A good nurse," wrote one student, "must be absolutely sterile."

703.   For all the story-books you read:
                   For all the pains you comforted:
                   For all you pitied, all you bore,
                   In sad and happy days of yore . . .
                   Take, nurse, the little book you hold
                        and remember me.

                                   —*Robert Louis Stevenson*

704.   The pretty young woman got her first job as a school nurse
in a local high school.

One day a boy reported to his teacher, "I think Tom is going to
be late to class, Mr. Jones. He has a medical problem."

"Oh," answered Mr. Jones, "has he seen the doctor?"

"No," replied the student, "but he sure got a good look at the
new nurse!"

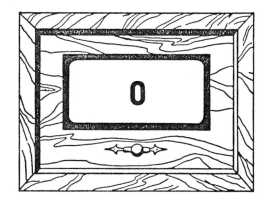

Opinion

705. The children were taken on their first trip to a museum, and in the Egyptian room, they gazed at a mummy over which hung a card on which was printed, "97 B.C."

"Children," asked the teacher, "does anyone know what that means?"

"I don't know for sure," said one tyke, "but it's my opinion that it's the number of the car that killed him."

706. One philosopher suggested that everyone on earth be made to wear a sign which states, "What I am about to say represents one two-billionth of the opinion of the world."

707. An error of opinion may be tolerated where reason is left free to combat it.

—Thomas Jefferson

708. A mass of men equals a mass of opinions.

—Ancient Latin Proverb

709. "Dear Miss Howard," wrote the small girl, "I am writing to tell you that I like you. I think you are a swell teacher. And I don't smell anything, no matter what Billy says!"

Opportunity

710. "What would you like to read if you were stranded on a desert island?" asked the creative writing teacher.
   Replied the sweet young thing, "A tattooed sailor."

711.   There is a tide in the affairs of men,
        Which, taken at the flood, leads on to fortune;
        Omitted, all the voyage of their life
        Is bound in shallows and in miseries.

—William Shakespeare

712. It seems men never moan over opportunities lost to do good, only the opportunities to be bad.

—Greek Proverb

Overachievement

713. The Lord's Prayer contains 56 words; Lincoln's Gettysburg Address, 260; The Ten Commandments, 300; The Declaration of

Independence, 3,000; a recent government order setting the price of cabbage—26,911.

714. The principal called the little girl to his office in order to congratulate her for selling the most tickets to the school play.

"You were so far ahead of all the other children," the principal remarked. "How did you ever do it?"

"Well, Sir," the girl answered, "I went up to each house with a big handful of tickets, and when the man or lady opened the door, I held out the tickets and said, 'Excuse me, but what are you doing on the night of May 23rd?' Everyone said that they were busy or had made plans for that night. That's when I said, 'Oh, that's great, 'cause our play is on the 24th!' "

715.
Awake, my soul! stretch every nerve
And press with vigour on;
A heavenly race demands thy zeal,
And an immortal crown.

—Philip Doddridge

716. Ah, but a man's reach should exceed his grasp,
Or what's a heaven for?

—Robert Browning

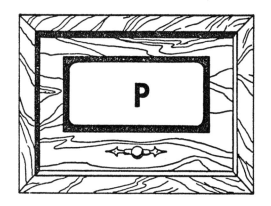

Parents

717. Parents are just one of those inconveniences with which children have to contend.

718. It's unfortunate but true—"Child Proof" and "Unbreakable" labels don't come on parents' hearts.

719. One sure sign that you are in an underdeveloped country is seeing the children there still obeying their parents.

720. A small boy came up to the school librarian's desk.
    "Excuse me," he asked, "but do you have any books for *kids* explaining *parents*?"

721. If the trend toward teenage marriages continues, this scene might well take place:

"Johnny, darling, I can't seem to do anything right. The baby keeps crying and crying, and I can't make it stop," wailed the teenage mother.

"Now, calm down, honey," said her equally young husband. "Just look in the book of instructions that came with him."

722. You are the bows from which your children as living arrows are sent forth.

—*Kahlil Gibran*

723.   And when with envy Time, transported,
                 Shall think to rob us of our joys,
                 You'll in your girls again be courted,
                 And I'll go wooing in my boys.

—*Thomas Percy*

724. The hardest thing for any adolescent to realize is that in another thirty years he'll be as stupid as his parents are now.

725. It was the first night that little Johnny was going to sleep without a night light in his room. Johnny ranted and raved in protest.

"Just settle down, son," said his father. "You're a big boy now. Besides, *I* haven't slept with a light on for years."

"Yeah, Daddy," whimpered the unconvinced little boy, "but you've got Mommy in there to protect you!"

726. Perhaps the little girl was on the right track when she wrote as her reason why parents fight with their children: "By the time our parents are parents, they are too old to change their habits."

Penmanship

727. The Principal's secretary was having a terrible time. Try as she might, she could not decipher the hastily scrawled note that the Principal had given her, telling her to make sure that she put it in the Daily Bulletin. She asked several teachers and the other secretaries, and no one could even begin to read it. Finally, she had an idea, and she walked into the Principal's office.

"Sir," she said, "you know that note you gave me this morning? Well, a breeze blew it out the window, so if you'll just dictate it, I'll take it down."

"Certainly," said the Principal, "it goes like this: 'To All Teachers: We have received several complaints about the quality of our students' written work. Please make every effort to teach proper penmanship at all levels.' "

728. Did you hear about the doctor who tried to hold up a bank, but the teller couldn't read his handwriting?

729. During a Parent-Teacher Conference, the mother commented on the blank space where her child's spelling mark should have been.

"Well, you see," explained the teacher, "I was just trying to be fair. Billy's handwriting is so bad I can't tell whether he can spell or not."

730. According to one lad, "Letters printed in a sloping type are said to be in hysterics."

731. Two boys were discussing their accomplishments.

"Why, I can do something that nobody else in the whole world can do," bragged one youth.

"What's that?" asked the other.

"I can read my own handwriting!"

732. "Now, Mary," said the teacher during a penmanship lesson, "why didn't you cross your 't'?"

"It's coming, Miss Jones," replied the little girl. "It's still in my pencil."

733. The Principal came storming out of his office.

"Who took this message?" he yelled at the office staff.

"I did," answered the student assistant.

"Why can't you write more legibly?"

"I would have," stammered the girl, "if the caller had spoken legibly."

People

734. Some people are like tea bags; you don't know their strength until you see them in hot water.

735. It's the nature of all people to believe that the hardships that befall them are a trial while the tragedies that befall others are judgments from God.

—19th Century American Proverb

736. The student must have been somewhat confused when he wrote: "An Octopus is a person who hopes for the best."

737. Popularity is the easiest thing to get and the hardest thing to keep.

—Will Rogers

738. We [the American People] view our atomic arsenal as proudly and as devotedly as any pioneer ever viewed his flintlock hanging over the mantel as his children slept and dreamed.

—William F. Buckley, Jr.

Perfection

739. The Principal was addressing his faculty as part of his campaign for 100% effeciency.

"Your classroom, this school, and, yes, even your home can be run efficiently. The secret is to take care of things as they occur and not to let them pile up or be put off.

"I always follow this philosophy," he continued. "Why, the very second something comes across my desk, I immediately give it to my secretary to do."

740. Every time a child is born into the world, it's Nature's attempt to make a perfect human being. Well, we've seen Nature pushing and contriving for some time now. We all know she's interested in quantity; but I think she's interested in quality, too.

—Thornton Wilder

741. Two young lovers were walking along the beach when the boy lifted his arm and joyously proclaimed, "Oh, Mighty and Majestic Ocean, roll your clear blue waves upon this waiting shore!"

His girl, caught up in the moment, pressed his other arm and said proudly, "Donald, you're wonderful! Just look—it's doing it!"

742. The husband and wife always argued over his unorthodox bridge playing. One night the man was delighted to have bid and made a grand slam. The wife, however, flattened his elation.

"If you had played that hand properly," she sanctimoniously remarked, "you'd never have made it!"

743.   Man is his own star; and that soul that can
          Be honest is the only perfect man.

—John Fletcher

744. Johnny was taken on his first trip to the West.

"There's the Grand Canyon, Johnny," pointed out his father.

The boy was thunderstruck by the awesome spectacle before him.

"Grand, nothing, Pop," he exclaimed. "That's perfect!"

745. His only fault is that he has no fault.

—*Pliny, the Younger*

746. Striving to be better, oft we mar what's well.

—*William Shakespeare*

Philosophy

747. One judge became concerned when he heard the prosecutor's case and decided to teach him a lesson.

"My dear fellow," said the judge, "your case is built on pure supposition. Sir, let me ask you a question. Let's say we had a horse here in the courtroom, and we said that his tail was another leg. How many legs would you suppose the horse then had?"

"Five," the lawyer promptly replied.

"So I thought," the judge answered sternly. "But, Sir, calling that tail a leg makes it neither right nor true."

748. A man came up to the next world. He saw the great sages of the past sitting on hard benches and studying. He complained to the angel on duty, "I just don't understand you people in heaven. Why aren't these great men in Paradise? They who did so much for mankind."

The angel looked puzzled.

"Paradise, what's that? I don't know what that means." And he kept uttering, "Paradise, what's that? What's that?"

The complainant tried to explain, "Paradise is a wonderful world, a reward for these great men, where they can enjoy the life in the world to come."

He continued to explain, and then the angel said, "Oh, I'm beginning to understand your concept of Paradise. You see these great ones—they are not in Paradise; Paradise is in them."

749. George Washington Carver, the famous black scientist whose research developed a multitude of uses for such humble crops as soy beans and peanuts, once told his philosophy of life in this story:

"When I was young I said to God, 'God, tell me the mystery of the universe.'

"But God answered, 'That knowledge is reserved for Me alone.'

"So I said, 'God, tell me the mystery of the peanut.'

"Then God said, 'Well, George, that's more nearly your size.' And He told me."

750. When the college student began to investigate the philosophies of the East, he decided that he should quit school and embark upon a life of meditation and teaching of philosophy.

He hired a room in a local hotel, sent out notices, and was soon ready to teach to a small group of students.

The day of his first class, he sat cross-legged on the floor and asked his students to do likewise. Then he began to chant and was soon in deep meditation. All at once, his eyes popped open and he shouted, "A sparrow does not fly in the light of the morning sun!"

"But," retorted one student, "sparrows *do* fly in the light of the morning sun."

"Silence!" shouted the young philosopher. "You are here to learn—not argue!"

751. "Trust and Love often go hand in hand," said the Minister to the young couple. "Let me tell you what I mean. Just this morning I went to get in my newspaper from the porch. It was raining, so I slipped on my wife's coat, since it was nearest to the door, you see. As I came out, the mailman kissed me. Well, I could only believe that the mailman's wife had a coat just like the one I had on."

752. There's no danger that mechanical devices and computer brains will replace man. Somebody will still have to pound the hell out of them to make them work.

753. The Philosopher has to be the bad conscience of his age.

—*Friedrich Nietzsche*

Physical Education

754. With the way educational thinking is today, is it any wonder that we spend half our tax money on a fleet of buses so the kids don't have to walk more than a block, and the other half on gyms and athletic equipment because they're not getting enough exercise.

755. As the coach walked around the practice field he noticed two boys, one of whom was exercising vigorously while the other put out only a half-hearted effort.

"Aren't you ashamed of yourself," the coach said to the slacking student. "Why, this young man is doing twice as much as you are."

"I know, Coach," the youth puffed, "I've been telling him that for the past twenty minutes, but he just refuses to slow down."

756. The coach was doing time trials when the principal walked by.

"I see you have a fine turnout for the Walking Club," said the principal.

"Walking Club, my eye," said the coach, "these are the best I could find for the hundred-yard dash!"

Plays

757. "Dad! Dad!" shouted the excited boy as he came home from school, "I got a part in the school play!"

"That's wonderful, son," replied his father. "What do you play?"

"It's a character part. I play an old man who is celebrating his 50th wedding anniversary. I've been married for fifty years."

"Married that long, hmmm?" mused the father. "Well, son, one of these days you'll get a speaking part."

758.   SCHOLAR EXPLAINING SHAKESPEARE

Enter first Lady-in-Waiting (Flourish,[1] Hautboys,[2] and[3] torches).[4]

First Lady-in-Waiting: What?[5] Ho![6] Where[7] is[8] the[9] music?[10]

Notes:

1. *Flourish*: The stage direction here is obscure. Clarke claims it should read, "Flarish," this changing the meaning of the passage to, "Flarish" (that is, the King's), but most authorities have agreed that it should remain "Flourish," supplying the predicate which is to be Flourished. There was at that time a custom in the countryside of England to flourish a mop as a signal to the passing vendor of berries, signifying that in that particular household there was a consumer demand for berries, and this may have been meant in this instance. That Shakespeare was cognizant of this custom of flourishing the mop for berries is shown in a similar passage in the second part of *King Henry IV*, where he has the Third Page enter and say, "Flourish." Cf. also *Hamlet*, IV, 7, iv.

—Robert Benchley

759.   Then there was the student who was such a poor actor, the only way he could get into a cast was to break his leg.

760.   It was a tradition of the high school that the senior class would present a Shakespearian play every year.

One graduate of that high school found himself at a faculty reception for the incoming freshmen at the college he planned to attend.

"My boy," asked a professor of English literature, "do you know William Shakespeare?"

"Know him!" exclaimed the lad, "Hell, he wrote our senior class play!"

761. All theories of what a good play is or how a good play should be written, are futile. A good play is a play which when acted upon the boards makes an audience interested and pleased. A play that fails in this is a bad play.

—Maurice Baring

762. The doctor's small son came running into his office one afternoon after school.

"Daddy!" he exclaimed, "I got it! I got it! Everybody in school wanted to play 'Tiny Tim' but I got it, 'cause the teacher said I had 'special qualifications.' "

"That's wonderful, son," said the doctor, "but what 'special qualifications' are you talking about?"

"I'm the only kid in class whose father can get him a crutch!"

Point of View

763. The young couple were down on their luck. Everything had turned against them, or so it seemed. Finally, they were down to their last few dollars, and they went to live with her parents in Las Vegas.

One day the desperate young man took the remaining money they had and went to the race track. After expenses he had exactly two dollars remaining. On a wild impulse he bet on the fifth horse in the fifth race who went off at fifty to one.

The horse won, and the young man bet all the money on the sixth horse in the sixth race who was at sixty to one. That horse won as well, and the young man left with a small fortune.

On his way home he couldn't resist dropping into a casino, and in half an hour he had taken in over one hundred and fifty thousand dollars!

Finally, and again on the sheerest instinct, he placed the entire fortune on number 31 on the roulette table. The wheel turned and the ball came to rest on number 32—he had lost everything!

When he returned home later that night, his wife began berating him for having gone to the track with the last of their money.

"What are you so upset about," stated the husband. "After all, I only lost two dollars."

764. When I hear people say they have not found the world and life so agreeable or interesting as to be in love with it, I am apt to think they have never been properly alive nor seen with clear vision the world they think so meanly of, or anything in it—not even a blade of grass.

—William Henry Hudson

765. The two teachers were talking in the school hallway.

"These shoes I'm wearing are going to be the death of me," said one woman.

"My dear," said her friend. "Why don't you slip them off? If you're sitting at your desk, no students will notice."

"Look," the first answered, "after school I have to get my car back from the garage and argue with the mechanic about the bill; then I have to do the shopping which I didn't do yesterday; then I'll go home and look at the bills the mailman has brought; then I'll have to clean up whatever the dog has knocked over during the day; then my husband is going to come home wanting dinner, and we will probably get into an argument."

"What has all that got to do with your shoes?" asked her friend.

"Just that the only pleasure I'm going to get all day long is taking them off," she answered, "and I'm going to save it until I really need it."

766. The first-grade teacher took her class to a matinee performance of a traveling circus that was passing through the area. Everything was going fine, and the children really seemed to enjoy the clowns, animals, and acrobats. Suddenly, however, the band began a heavily rhythmical beat and a chorus line of shapely beauties appeared, clad only in the briefest possible swatches of red and gold material. Slowly, they began to undulate in time to the music.

The flustered teacher sat frozen in her chair. What had she done? What would the children think of this highly inappropriate entertainment? She was at a loss to think of what to do.

The children came alive and began bouncing up and down in their seats, pointing fingers at the dancing girls and whispering to each other.

Finally, one little boy made his way to the teacher.

"The kids wanted me to ask you if you see that," he said excitedly. "Those ladies are wearing our school colors!"

767.   The teacher asked her class to name the days of the week.

One little future homemaker replied, "Washing, Ironing, Cooking, Cleaning, Shopping, Mending, and Beauty Parlor!"

768.   The husband always made it a point to give his wife some bit of good news each night when he came home from the office. One day, his wife had had a rather hectic time, and she said as he came in, "Honey, do I need your good news tonight."

"Well, dear, you know how you have a lot of helpers around the house like the washing machine, the vacuum cleaner, the garbage disposal, and me?"

"I know," she said with a loving smile.

"Well," he said, "all the machines are still working."

769.   A teacher from one of the Plain's states was visiting a friend who taught in a town nestled in the Rocky Mountains. This teacher took his friend to visit the school in which he taught. His room overlooked a verdant valley with several magnificent purple mountains in the background.

"How about that!" exclaimed the teacher from the mountains.

"Hmmm," murmured the teacher from the plains, "that would sure be some view if you could only get those mountains out of the way."

770. One teacher tells of the indomitable spirit of one of her charges who had left his lunch at home, broken the zipper on his snow suit, fallen down and ripped his trousers, scraped his knee on the playground, and finally took a headlong plunge down the stairs during a fire drill.

As the teacher was picking him up and brushing him off, the youth was smiling happily.

"Look," he said, holding up a scratched and begrimed hand, "I found a dime when I fell. This is my lucky day."

771. On the block near the school there were two houses. In the front yard of one, there was a little tot who was always screaming and pounding on the gate to go out. In the front yard of the other house, however, an equally young child was always seen happily playing with his toys.

The teacher who had to walk past this scene every day on her way to school, stopped one afternoon at the house of the screamer and inquired of his mother the reason for the continual upset.

"Oh," his mother said, "I told him that I locked the gate so he couldn't get out, and that upset him, so he carries on like that."

Immediately the teacher went to the house of the calm child and asked the reason for the gentle behavior.

"It's simple," said that lad's mother, "I told him that the gate was locked to keep the other children out."

Poise

772. The Chairman of the Science Department at the local high school, the principal of the school, and the district Superintendent of Schools, were friends and for years enjoyed a Friday night poker game. One Friday, however, an overzealous rookie spotted them through an open living room window and arrested them for gambling. They were taken down to headquarters and immediately brought before the night court judge.

"Mr. Jones!" exclaimed the judge, "why, you have my son in class. Were you playing cards for money?"

Thinking of the shame that might attend conviction, the teacher took a deep breath and lied, "No, sir, I was not."

"And you, Mr. Smith," the judge continued. "You are the principal of the high school; a leader of youth. Don't tell me you were playing cards for money?"

With a furtive look toward heaven, Mr. Smith sighed, "No, Your Honor, I was not."

"And Mr. Baker," said the judge as he addressed the Superintendent of Schools, "were *you* playing cards for money?"

The Superintendent looked about him, spread his hands palm up, and asked, "With whom?"

773. Beauty without grace is the hook without the bait.

—Ralph Waldo Emerson

774. The grass stoops not, she treads on it so light.

—William Shakespeare

775. Grace is that quality which, if a woman has it, she doesn't need anything else, and if she doesn't, nothing else will do.

—Sir James M. Barrie

Politics

776. Practical politics consists in ignoring facts.

—Henry Adams

777. Mayor Smith was visiting the school, and he stopped into one classroom where a group of third grade students were being quizzed by their teacher.

"Who is responsible for our lovely new school?" she asked.

"Mayor Smith!" came the response.

"Who gave us the marvelous new athletic stadium?"

"Mayor Smith!"

"Who makes the sun rise in the morning?"

"God!" shouted one child.

"That does it!" exclaimed Mayor Smith from the back of the room. "I ain't stayin' in no place with an opposition candidate."

778. "Johnny, what do you think Thomas Jefferson was noted for?"

"I think it was his memory, Mrs. Davis. He could remember everything."

"Why do you say that?"

"Well, I saw a whole building named for it—The Jefferson Memory-All."

779. A straw vote only shows which way the hot air blows.

—*O. Henry*

780. Politics is the science of how who gets what, when and why.

—*Sidney Hillman*

781. "And who is the Speaker of the House?" asked the civics teacher.

Answered one student, "My mother!"

782. Those who would treat politics and morality apart will never understand the one or the other.

—*Rousseau*

783. "You understand," said the teacher, "that as Class Secretary, you are responsible for keeping the minutes of the class meetings."

"Yes, Ma'am," said little Kathy. "I can do it all right."

At the next class meeting, the teacher said, "And now, I'd like Kathy to give us the minutes of the last meeting."

"Twenty-three," said Kathy.

784.   When quacks with pills political would dope us,
             When politics absorbs the live-long day,
             I like to think about the star Canopus,
             So far, so far away!

—Bert Leston Taylor

Prejudice

785.   There are times when a bigot is any person who espouses an idea with which you don't happen to agree.

786.   He flattered himself on being a man without any prejudices; and this pretention itself is a very great prejudice.

—Anatole France

787.   Prejudices, it is well known, are most difficult to eradicate from the heart whose soil has never been loosened or fertilized by education.

—Charlotte Bronte

788.   The teacher called the group of children around him on the playground. In his hand he held a bunch of helium-filled balloons which twisted and strained to be free. Without comment, he let a red balloon, a white, balloon, a yellow balloon, and a black balloon go free. Together they rode the wind and mounted into the sky.

"You see," the teacher said as he pointed heavenward, "it isn't the color; it's what's inside that counts."

Principal

789. The principal called his faculty together and outlined a complete plan for the reorganization of the school.

After an hour-long speech, he concluded, "Finally, I want you to know that what I've said here today is only a suggestion. Not one of you has to go along with it. In fact, anyone who is opposed to my plan may indicate so by merely raising his hand and saying, 'I quit.' "

790. A mountaineer brought his son into school to enroll him.

"I wants my boy to git some learnin'," he told the principal. "Whatcha got?"

"Sir," said the principal, "we offer English, science, math courses like trigonometry, and . . ."

"That's it!" interrupted the hillbilly. "Give him some of that there trigger-nometry. He's the worst shot in the family."

791. "Does your wife know that you're bringing me home for dinner?" the principal asked the department chairman.

"Of course she does," he answered. "We argued about it all last night."

792. And then there's the principal who keeps a bowl of goldfish on his desk because he wants something around him that opens its mouth without complaining or yelling about something.

Problems

793. It was terrible. Every single night during dinner there was a family argument. The father was always caught in the middle. One night he'd had enough.

"Look!" he exclaimed, "I'm just the father here, but when is somebody going to listen to what I want?"

At this point his little son tugged on his sleeve and said, "Daddy, it would help if you cried a little."

794.   Then there was the teacher who fainted when his son asked for the garage keys and came out with the lawn mower.

795.   The future belongs to the young, and with the shape the world is in, they're welcome to it.

796.   The two school custodians were struggling with the new sink for the science lab. As much as they struggled and huffed and puffed, the sink remained immobile. Finally, they set it down in the doorway and looked at each other.

"That's it, Bill," said one. "I don't see any way that we are going to get that sink in through this door."

"In?" exclaimed Bill. "I thought I was helping you take it out!"

797.   The biggest problem in the world
Could have been solved when it was small.

—*Witter Bynner*

Professors

798.   "We have to get rid of this cat," said the professor's wife. "I want you to take her out into the country somewhere and lose her."

The professor started off with the animal. Much later, the wife heard a noise and investigated, only to find the professor sitting in the living room, stroking the cat.

"She stays," said the professor.

"You old softie," said his wife. "I bet you never even turned her loose."

"You're wrong," answered the professor. "In fact, if I hadn't followed her home, I'd still be lost.

799. The Chairman of the Board of Directors and a couple of professors were arguing that if the salary guide didn't get better, it would become harder and harder to attract learned teachers to their university.

One of the newest members of the faculty spoke up at this point.

"I don't know," he said. "I was just hired as the new English professor, and I don't think youse guys knows what your talking about."

800. A college professor is a guy who gets paid from what's left over in the athletic budget.

801. The professor was known as an ardent fisherman. One day, his class got him talking about his favorite hobby.

"I even dream about it," he told his students. "Just last night I had a dream that I was in a velvet-lined boat in the middle of a placid lake with a beautiful harem-girl."

"Wow, professor," commented one student, "that's some dream. How did it turn out?"

"Oh," the professor said, "I caught a six-pound bass."

802. Two professors were sitting in the exclusive, heretofore all-male University Club commiserating with each other over the new rule permitting women on the premises for the first time.

"They're going to let wives in here for dining and dancing in the evening," said one professor shaking his head sadly.

'But we have some members who aren't married," pondered the other. "I wonder if they can bring their girl friends?"

"Well, I suppose if she were the wife of one of the members," said the first, "it would be all right."

Psychologist, The School

803.   A student reported to the school psychologist for an interview.

"Young man," said the psychologist, "are you bothered by improper thoughts?"

"Gosh, no," replied the student. "In fact, I'm rather fond of them."

804.   The school psychologist walked into the study hall to find several boys sitting there assiduously doing their homework while one boy sat with his chair tilted back, gazing wistfully out the window.

"Young man," said the psychologist, "don't you take this opportunity to do your homework?"

"I never do homework," said the boy, "but, you see, I've adjusted to failure."

805.   The school psychologist came home to find her son standing in the bathroom up to his ankles in water. Not wanting to jump to conclusions, the woman stood, pondering what to do.

Her son looked up and seemed to read her thoughts.

"Mom," he said, "this is no time for analysis. It's time for a mop!"

806.   The school psychologist was addressing the PTA meeting. It had come time for the question and answer session, and one woman asked, "Sir, what do you think is the principal psychological concern of children today."

"Same as it was yesterday," replied the psychologist. "Mothers!"

807.   "I understand your last job was as secretary to a school psychologist," said the prospective employer to the applicant. "Why did you leave that position?"

"I just couldn't stand it any longer," she said. "If I was late, I was showing hostile tendencies; if I was early, I was having feelings of anxiety; and if I was on time, that meant I was being compulsive."

808. "Madam," said the school psychologist to the mother of the obstreperous child, "you need help as much as your child. You're overwrought. You need to relax. I'll see Billy in one week. During that time, I want *you* to take a drink of liquor at least once a day. It will help your nerves."

The following week saw Billy and his mother back in the psychologist's office. Mother went in first.

"And how is Billy making out?" the man asked.

"Billy?" slurred the woman as she slumped in her chair, "Who's Billy?"

PTA

809. When Mrs. Smith gave birth to her eighth child, she received a phone call in the hospital from the president of the PTA, congratulating her on the birth. Mrs. Smith began to cry.

"What is it, my dear?" inquired the PTA President. "Is something wrong with the baby?"

"The baby's fine," Mrs. Smith whimpered. "It's just that it suddenly occurred to me with frightening clarity that I'm *never* going to get out of the PTA!"

810. "Mary," asked the woman, "is your son better behaved in school this year?"

"Let me put it this way," said her friend, "I'm still going to PTA meetings, but I'm going under an assumed name."

811. "Hey, Mom," said the youth as he came in from school, "Guess what? You're invited to a parent-faculty get-together that is going to be an intimate gathering."

"What do you mean, 'intimate gathering?' " she asked.

"Well," he answered, "so far it's just you, the principal, the English teacher, and me."

812.   Comes the day when my children can say,
                "I'm married." Oh, what a great day!
                I'll give in to my wish
                To do nothing but fish,
                And let them start their own PTA!

Questions

813. "Billy," asked the teacher, "how long did the Revolutionary War last?"

"From page 73 until page 145," answered Billy.

814. "Mary" asked the teacher, "how do you spell 'bombastic?' "

"The same way everybody else spells it," answered Mary.

815. Them that asks no questions isn't told a lie.

—Rudyard Kipling

816.   I like rivers
Better than oceans, for we see both sides.
An ocean is forever asking questions
And writing them aloud along the shore.

—Edwin Arlington Robinson

817.   The Minister had just completed his lesson about "turning the other cheek" to the littlest members of his congregation.

"Now children," he asked, "why do we not hit someone who has hit or insulted us?"

" 'Cause," answered one little boy, "they're all bigger than us!"

818.   "Boy, was the teacher upset today," said Johnny. "He kept asking the same question, and no one could give him an answer."

"Well, Johnny," said his mother, "it must have been very difficult. What was it?"

"Who let the air out of his tires?"

819.   The teacher asked his students to write a list of the nine greatest Americans. All the class had finished with their lists except Johnny.

"Johnny, what's taking you so long?"

"I'm sorry," Johnny answered. "I can't decide who the pitcher should be."

820.   The young teacher was about to be married, and at the wedding rehearsal it was evident that she was a mass of nerves.

"I have this fear," she exclaimed, "that the Minister will ask if I take this man, and I won't know what to say."

"Oh, come on," chided her Maid of Honor. "When you're in school, you know all the answers."

"That's true," said the teacher bride. "But then, in school, I'm the one asking the questions."

821. Life is nothing more than a series of people questioning where we are going—our mothers, our wives, and those attending our funeral.

Quick Thinking

822. "I think that completes all the forms and papers," said the school secretary to the new teacher. "There's just one more item we must know. Whom shall we notify in the event of an accident?"

"The nearest first-aid squad," answered the honest educator.

823. The two teachers were speeding along the highway when they were pulled over by a patrolman.

"Honestly, Officer," lied the driver, "I'm a doctor, and I'm rushing my patient to a sanitorium."

Suspiciously, the policeman looked over at the passenger.

"Officer," said the other teacher, "I told him not to speed. After all, we'd get there faster if we just flapped our arms and flew."

They didn't get the ticket.

824. The honors for quick thinking combined with saving face have to go to the young ROTC captain who took his squad out on field maneuvers and accidentally tramped them through the prize tulip beds of the college president.

"You blithering idiot!" stormed the president. "You nincompoop!"

Completely speechless with rage, the president stamped away.

After he had gone, the ROTC captain pulled himself up to his full height, and turned to his men.

"I'm sure glad he used the right passwords," said the youth, "or I'd have never let him pass."

825. The teacher took her class on a tour of a candy factory. After the tour, the factory representative took the children to a reception where a huge bowl of candy dominated the center of the room.

"I want each of you to reach in and take a handful for your-self," the guide told the children.

With squeals of delight, they all fell upon the candy, all but one little boy who stood apart from the others, his hands in his pockets.

"Would you like me to get you some candy, son," asked the kindly guide.

The little boy shook his head, and the man reached in and poured a generous helping into the child's pocket.

On their way out of the factory, the teacher remarked that she had never seen the child so shy before.

"Are you kidding?" quipped the child. "His hands were big-ger than mine."

826. "Honey," said the teacher's wife who was about to go shopping, "Sally just got a new dress!"

Picturing their already over-extended budget, her husband, thinking fast, said, "Darling, I'm such a lucky man. My wife is so beautiful she doesn't need new clothes to look great."

827. The sociology professor asked his class if they could deter-mine which group of people produced the most children.

One pretty coed quickly answered, "Women!"

828. "Billy," asked the math teacher, "if you had three choco-late bars, and I asked you for two of them, how many would you have?"

"Three," Billy answered truthfully.

Reading

829. The Thanskgiving holiday was almost at hand, and it had been decided that Junior was old enough to do the carving and dutifully impress the assembled relatives. The only trouble with the scheme was that Junior hadn't the slightest idea of how to go about the process.

Mother finally bought him a book which described what he should do in complete detail.

"Just read it," she instructed, "and follow what it says precisely."

On the big day, with relatives in attendance, Junior rose, took carving knife and fork in hand, and addressed the bird. That's all he did, however, for he stood frozen to the spot as relatives began to shift uneasily in their chairs, and father began to turn red.

"Junior," whispered Mother, "do what you read in the book!"

"I'm trying to, Mom," came his stage-whispered answer, "but I can't find the dotted lines!"

830.   Reading maketh a full man, conference a ready man, and writing an exact man.

—*Francis Bacon*

831.   Mother went to school to find out why little Harry had failed the history test.

"For one thing, Mrs. Jones," the teacher remarked during the conference, "Harry didn't know when Washington and Lincoln died."

"Is that really so bad?" inquired Harry's mother. "After all, his father and I hardly ever read the obituaries either."

832.   The book which you read from a sense of duty, or because for some reason you must, doesn't usually make friends with you.

—*William Dean Howells*

833.   The two children waited patiently until the reading lesson was over. Then they both asked to be excused at the same time.

Standing in the boys' lavatory, they fixed their eyes on the wall as their lips began to move silently. Finally, one youth's eyes grew wide.

"I told you!" he exclaimed. "It is so a dirty word!"

834.   "I think this here whole education thing is unnecessary," said the old codger to the principal at the open school session.

"How can you say a thing like that?" demanded the principal.

"Look," the oldster replied, "when I was a boy they give me all sorts of books and told me I had to learn how to read them. Then the next thing you know, they goes and invents television and makes the whole danged thing unnecessary!"

Relatives

835.   Fate makes our relatives; choice makes our friends.

—Jacques Delille

836.   The people people work with best
                Are sometimes very queer;
                The people people own by birth
                Quite shock your first idea.
                The people people have for friends
                Your common sense appall,
                But the people people marry
                Are the queerest folk of all.

—Charlotte P. S. Gilman

837.   Sitting in their seashore cottage, the teacher and his wife were talking.

"You know, dear," said the wife, "this is the first year we haven't been deluged with either my relatives or yours. However did you do it?"

"I took some advice that my principal gave me," replied her husband. "I borrowed money from the rich ones and lent it to the poor ones, and we haven't seen any of them since!"

838.   The thermostat in the living room was defective, and the teacher had meant to get it fixed but could never seem to find the time. One night, it gave up the ghost, and as a result the furnace shut down and refused to start up.

When the furnace repair man arrived the next morning, the teacher took him into the living room where his wife stood waiting by the defective thermostat.

"Before you look at the furnace," the teacher said, "I'd like you to meet the cause of all my troubles."

"Ma'am," said the repair man as he tipped his hat, "it's a pleasure to make your acquaintance."

839. "If you weren't so lazy you'd be principal of the school by now!" chided the little old lady. "And, Madge, these eggs are cold. You always were a terrible cook. I'm going up to my room!"

After she had left, the teacher turned to his wife and said, "I swear, Madge, one of these days your mother is going to go too far!"

"*My* mother," said Madge, "I thought she was *your* mother!"

840. Mary was giving her teacher a book for her birthday and wanted to write something in it. She looked through her parent's library and found an inscription in one of her mother's cookbooks.

Imagine her teacher's surprise when she opened Mary's gift, a beautiful leather-bound Bible, and read: "Dearest Madam, I hope this book will add spice to your life. Best Wishes from The Author."

Report Card

841. The teenaged girl stormed into the house after school one day and flourished her report card under her mother's nose.

"Just look at this!" she exclaimed. "Look at that box marked 'SEX.' They gave me an 'F' in it, and they didn't even tell me I was taking the course!"

842. Johnny walked up to the teacher's desk and whispered, "Mrs. Smith, I gotta talk to you. I like you a lot, so I'm gonna warn you. You're in a lot of trouble. My mother said if I got another report card like my last one, somebody was gonna get skinned alive!"

843. One little guy probably headed off a good spanking when he came home with a disastrous report card by asking, "Mom, do you think my problem could possibly be hereditary?"

844. Then there was the daughter of the professional actor who told her father that he should be very happy. She had just gotten her report card, and she was being held over for another season.

845. "Well, I think we have last semester's problem licked," the husband told his wife as he looked over his son's failing report card. "With these grades, Johnny couldn't possibly be cheating."

Respect

846.
Here's one of the rules
That we learn just by living:
Respect is a thing
That is gotten by giving.

847. For her high school graduation, Daddy got his daughter a string of genuine pearls.

"How marvelous," remarked the girl. "And to think that these come from a slimy little creature."

"Hold it!" said Dad. "If there's one thing I demand, it's respect!"

848. To be capable of respect is almost as rare as to be worthy of it.

—Joseph Joubert

Responsibility

849. Liberty means responsibility. That's why most people dread it.

—George Bernard Shaw

850. The college professor says, "These students are woefully unprepared. What did they do with them in high school?"

The high school teacher says, "Look at these terrible scores! Didn't they teach them anything in elementary school?"

The elementary educator says, "My goodness, didn't that kindergarten teacher prepare these children for school?"

The kindergarten teacher says, "This child is impossible! What must his mother be like?"

And the mother says, "Don't blame me! Have you seen his father's side of the family?"

851. The sign said, "Responsible Boy Wanted."

The young man who applied remarked to his prospective employer, "This job's for me. The last place I worked, a lot of things went wrong, and I was always responsible!"

852. The two youngsters on the class trip to the Modern Art Museum rounded a corner and came face to face with a modern sculpture composed of various shapes of scrap iron welded together.

"Quick," said one of them, "let's rejoin the group before somebody says *we* broke it!"

Retirement

853. That happy age when a man can be idle with impunity.

—Washington Irving

854. When the two teachers retired, they took all the money they had saved over the years and decided to buy a cattle ranch.

"We'd like to buy two hundred cows," they told the cattle supply operator, "and two hundred bulls."

"Excuse me," said the man somewhat daintily, "but you really only need one bull."

The one teacher turned to the other and then back to the agent.

"We know," the educator said, "but we also know what it is to be lonely."

855. Said the teacher who was about to retire to his still-working colleague: "I look at it this way—I'm not retired, I'm retreaded."

856. On the occasion of his seventieth birthday, Mark Twain remarked, "It's a long stretch between that first birthday speech and this one. That was my cradle song, and this is my swan song, I suppose. I'm used to swan songs; I've sung them several times before.''

Reunion, The Class

857. When a person attends his class reunion after twenty-five years, he should be prepared for the fact that his classmates will probably be so bald, fat, and nearsighted that they will have trouble recognizing him.

858. "Daddy," said the man's teen-aged daughter, "I want to talk to you."

"Sure, honey, what is it?"

"I want to know how you can do this to mother? I think it's horrible enough to spend the weekend with another woman, but to be so cruel as to tell mother about it . . ."

". . . Another woman . . .weekend . . ." babbled the shocked man, "What are you talking about?"

"You thought I didn't hear," she answered, "but I listened. You were telling mother that you were going to spend the weekend at your girlfriend's place. What's her name? Alma . . . oh, yes . . . Alma Mater!''

859.   EULOGY FOR A CLASS REUNION

(In the following, fill in the blanks as they apply to your particular class.)

It has been a little more than _____ years since we last met as a class at _____ upon the occasion of our graduation. It is inevitable, that in that span of years, many of our teachers and classmates will have been taken from us.

It is, therefore, altogether fitting and proper, that we should pause in this hour of levity and reflect in our own lives the memory of those who have died.

I ask that we now bow our heads in silent meditation, and each in his own way pay tribute to the memory of those who do not answer when their name is called.

(As heads are bowed, recite the following:)

Now the hour of reunion has arrived,
In this room of mirth and cheer;
And silence descends from heaven,
Upon the group assembled here.
Slowly die the fire's last embers,
As the night grows still and serene;
And we toast our absent classmates,
Who have passed beyond the screen.
We behold with eyes grown older,
With eyes that have a magic scope;
Life's abandoned fires that smolder,
On the distant trail of hope.
And our memory is beguiling,
When the lights are soft and low;
For we see our classmates smiling,
As they smiled long years ago.
So to you our absent classmates,
With our hearts and hands held high;
We drink a toast to your memory,
That will never, never die.

—*Dr. Chester B. Ralph*

School, The

860. The fourth-grade pupil was counselling his younger brother who was getting ready to enter school.

"Just remember one thing," he said. "School is not like home. When the teacher says 'No,' she means it."

861. School days are the best days of your life—especially if you're a mother with children old enough to go there.

862. "Now that you have spelled it correctly," said the teacher, "can you use the word 'hypocrite' in a sentence?"

"The boy was a hypocrite," answered one lad, "when he smiled as he entered school."

863. The little first-grader came home from his first day in school.

"How did it go today?" asked his mother

"It wasn't as bad as I thought it was going to be," replied her son. "This strange man wanted to know how to spell 'dog,' so I told him."

864. "Before you start thinking that school is terrible," said the teacher to the unhappy student, "just remember that 'now' are 'the good old days' you'll be reminiscing about with *your* children."

865.   Better build schoolrooms for "the boy"
            Than cells and gibbets for "the man."

—Eliza Cook

866. Mother was waiting for Betty as she returned from her first day in school.

"Well," said mother, "what did you learn?"

"I don't think I learned enough," answered Betty, "they want me to come back tomorrow."

Science

867. Where the telescope ends, the microscope begins. Which of the two has the grander view?

—Victor Hugo

868. A question on a science test was, "What is the difference between lightning and electricity?"

Answered the worldly-wise student, "You don't have to pay for lightning."

869. Every great advance in science has come from one source—imagination.

—John Dewey

870. Men love to wonder, and that's the seed of science.

—Ralph Waldo Emerson

871. Scientists can tell you just to the minute when something is going to happen ten million miles away, but none of them has ever been smart enough to tell you what day to put on your heavy underwear.

—Will Rogers

872. "Class," said the science teacher, "can anyone tell me what 'nitrates' are?"

"Sure," answered one of his students with a smile, "about half as expensive as day rates."

873. Science is simply common sense at its best.

—Thomas Huxley

874. "What happened during the lunar eclipse last night?" asked the teacher.

"Gosh, Mrs. Jones, I don't know," said Timmy. "It was so dark out I couldn't see anything."

875. Two cows were grazing alongside a highway when a milk truck passed by. On the side of the truck was a sign that read, "Pasteurized, Homogenized, Standardized, Vitamins A and D added."

One cow turned to the other and said, "Makes you feel sort of inadequate, doesn't it?"

Secretary, The School

876. "Is the principal in?" asked the caller.

"Are you a salesman, parent, or a friend of his?" asked the school secretary.

"All three," replied the visitor.

"Well, then, he's in a department meeting; he's out of town; and won't you step in and see him?"

877. The first clue the principal had that the secretary was new at her job was when she asked him if he wanted the carbon paper double spaced too.

878. The principal called the school secretary into his office.

"Ms. Jones," he said, "I'd like you to know that you are an attractive and intelligent young lady. The faculty and the student body find you personable, affable, and a calming influence in times of trouble."

"Why . . . why, thank you," blushed the young lady.

"That's quite all right," said the principal. "I just felt you should know that, because we are now going to discuss your shorthand and typing!"

879. "I think the principal likes me," the school secretary told her friend. "Today he gave me a gift."

"A gift!" said the friend. "What was it?"

"A dictionary," the secretary replied.

880. The school secretary was quite efficient, but she sometimes shocked the principal by the low-cut or high-hemmed outfits she wore. One day, he called her into his office.

"Ms. Thomas," he began, "you work in a school. I really think that when you dress for work you should try to show a little more decorum."

"Really, sir," she exclaimed. "I do have my limits. What I'm wearing now is as far as I go!"

881. "Young man," said the principal to the persistent salesman, "I distinctly heard my secretary tell you I was out. What made you think I was here?"

"That was easy, sir," said the salesman brightly. "Your secretary was busy."

882. "Miss Jones, why are you always late?" stormed the principal to his secretary. "You'd better have a good reason."

"I do," answered the secretary. "It's the only way I can make the day go faster."

Self-Improvement

883. Then there was the hillbilly family who sent their son off to school. One day he came running up to their mountain cabin shouting joyously.

"Maw! Paw!" he exclaimed. "I done learned to write!"

With that he took a piece of birch bark and a lump of coal and wrote something.

"We'uns is might proud of you," said Paw. "What's that say?"

"I don't rightly know, Paw," answered the son. "We won't learn how to read for another month."

884. The young teacher picked up the phone and dialed the local elementary school.

"Excuse me," he said, "but do you have any openings for sixth-grade teachers? . . . Oh, you have a sixth-grade teacher . . .

How is he making out? . . . He's that good, huh? . . . O.K., thanks anyway.''

"Looking for a job?'' asked someone who had overheard.

"Oh, no,'' the other replied. "I *am* the sixth grade teacher at that school. I just like to check up from time to time to see how I'm doing.''

885.   "I hear Jane is marrying a self-made man.''

"Yes. I met him, and all I can say is that I hope she doesn't have too hard a time making the alterations.''

Service

886.   "You must be like the little ant,'' the Sunday School teacher told the children. "You must work hard day in and day out. You must never take time for your own concerns, but must work for the good of others. You must labor long, thankless, tiresome hours. And, like the little ant, do you know what you'll get for all your effort?''

"Sure,'' answered one child. "Stepped on!''

887.   At a very exclusive restaurant, an educator-on-the-town asked if there was any wild rice available.

"No, sir,'' replied the haughty waiter, "but if the gentleman wishes, I will find some tame rice and aggravate it for him.''

888.   The little rich boy had proven a real problem for the school. No matter what was presented to the lad, it was never good enough, and by noon of the first day he had scorned his teachers, classmates, desk, room, and locker. Now it was time for lunch, and the harried teacher took the class to the cafeteria.

Naturally, the boy began to complain. That salad didn't look fresh enough, there weren't enough desserts, etc. Finally, the lad remarked that they were not serving any seafood, which was something he particularly liked.

"Don't they serve crabs here?'' he asked his teacher.

"Harold," the teacher replied, "they serve anybody, now sit down and eat!"

889. They also serve who only stand and wait.

—John Milton

890. He profits most who serves best.

—Motto of Rotary International

891. As soon as public service ceases to be the chief business of the citizens, and they would rather serve with their money than with their persons, the State is not far from its fall.

—Jean Jacques Rousseau

892. Then there was the teacher who singlehandedly rescued a child from a burning bus. The next day the boy's mother arrived to ask the teacher what she had done with the boy's lunchbox.

Sex Education

893. "Hey, Pop!" shouted the boy as he came in from school. "Today the teacher told us all about the birds and the bees."

"Oh . . . er . . . well, son . . ." stammered the father, ". . . I . . . I think its a good thing for you to know about . . . Sex, I mean . . ."

"Heck, Pop," responded the boy, "I know all about that sex stuff. I mean we started nature study, and the teacher told us about the birds and the bees!"

894. One teacher was flabbergasted when she overheard one of her students, a very cute little five-year-old girl, giving a lecture on where babies come from, complete with the correct anatomical names. Several other youngsters were avidly listening. Finally, one little boy spoke up.

"Nancy," he said, "you've got it all wrong. The stork finds the baby under a cabbage leaf and brings it to the Mommies and Daddies."

"I know that," Nancy answered solemnly, "but Daddy doesn't. That's why he made up this story."

895. The little boys were playing when they found a kitten.

"Is it a boy cat or a girl cat?" asked one tyke.

"I don't know," answered the other. "Let's take it to my mother. She'll tell us."

They did just that, and mother turned the kitten on its back, took a quick glance, and announced, "It's a boy kitten."

"How does she know it's a boy cat?" one child asked later.

"She's very good at it," commented the other. "She can tell by the way the hair grows on the belly."

896. "Well," said the father to his teen-aged son, "how did the first day of that new Sex Education class go? What have you learned so far?"

"I learned three things, Dad," said the boy. "I learned that there are men; I learned that there are women; and I learned that if you laugh at either of the first two facts you get sent to the office."

897. Johnny came home from school all excited.

"We're gonna have a course in Sex Education this year," he announced.

"That's fine, son," said his father. "If you have any questions, I'll be glad to answer them for you."

"I don't know, Dad," said Johnny. "You didn't do so well with compound fractions."

Speakers

898. The meeting of the teacher's association was almost over except for Mayor Smith who was to be the guest speaker of the evening. Everyone knew they were in for it when the Mayor pulled out a gargantuan typed manuscript and began to read it in a dull and nasal tone.

Several teachers attempted to make hasty exits, and this was bad enough, but the association president noticed that the vice-president was beginning to fall asleep on the dais. As surreptitiously as possible, he reached over and tapped the offender with his gavel.

"Is it over?" he yelled as he jerked upward. Then, seeing the Mayor still speaking, he exclaimed, "Do it again and put me out till he's over!"

899. Many speakers who rise to the occasion should have remained seated.

900. Most after-dinner speakers follow the same formula: Five minutes of wheat diluted by twenty-five minutes of chaff.

901. Catching his breath in the middle of a lengthy harangue on the needs of today's education, the speaker at the educator's conference proclaimed, "I am a a man of few words!"

"That may be!" shouted one of his fellow educators, "but you're sure worrying the hell out of the ones you do know!"

902. Some speakers are like gunfighters in the Old West; they shoot from the hip without taking aim.

Speaking

903. Adam was the only man who, when he said a good thing, knew that nobody had said it before him.

—*Mark Twain*

904.   You'd scarce expect one of my age
To speak in public on the stage;

And if I chance to fall below
Demosthenes or Cicero,
Don't view me with a critic's eye,
But pass my imperfections by,
Large streams from little fountains flow,
Tall oaks from little acorns grow.

—David Everett

905. One teacher we know claims that "monologue" may be defined as an argument between a husband and a wife.

906. The best advice on how to save face is to remember to keep the lower half shut.

907. If someone says, "It goes without saying . . ." you can be sure he's not going to let it.

908. If you want to give a successful speech, remember this maxim: Engage brain before speaking.

Spelling

909. "The secret of success, my boy," said the Superintendent to the principal, "is to hire a secretary who can spell all those big words you'll be using."

910. I don't give a damn for a man that can spell a word only one way.

—Mark Twain

911.   We drove the Indians out of the land,
But a dire revenge these redmen planned,
For they fastened a name to every nook,
And every boy with a spelling book

Will have to toil till his hair turns gray
Before he can spell them the proper way.

—*Eva March Tappan*

912.   Johnny's mother knew what a terrible letter-writer her son was, so she came up with a rather ingenious plan. She gave him several postcards, already addressed, and told him to drop one in the mail every day or so with just the words "I'm fine" on them. Then she packed him off to camp.

When no card arrived for several days, she began to worry. Finally, after a week with no word, she phoned the camp to see what was the matter.

"Why haven't we heard from you, Johnny?" she demanded. "Are you sick or something?"

"No, Mom," came the reply. "I'm all right. I just couldn't spell 'miserable.' "

913.   One of the questions on the test was, "Why is 'PSYCHOL-OGY' spelled with a 'P'?"

Mary thought and thought and finally wrote, "I'm psure I don't know, but maybe it might psound psort of psilly without it."

914.   The heart of our trouble is with our foolish alphabet. It doesn't know how to spell, and it can't be taught.

—*Mark Twain*

915.   The teacher was getting tired of the myriad of spelling errors his students were making on their papers.

"Class, from now on, if you don't know how to spell a word, look it up in the dictionary."

The age-old lament came from the back of the room.

"Sir, if I don't know how to spell it, how can I find the word in the dictionary?"

"That's simple," said the teacher. "Just ask me how to spell it, and *then* you can look it up."

916.   The schoolteacher was taking her first golfing lesson.

"Is the word spelled P-U-T or P-U-T-T?" she asked the instructor.

"P-U-T-T is correct," he replied. "*Put* means to place a thing where you want it. *Putt* means merely a vain attempt to do the same thing."

Sports

917.   In olden times there were no athletics. In those rough days each man carried his athletics at the hilt of his sword or the butt of his quarterstaff. After a game, one side didn't play any more.

—*Stephen Leacock*

918.   At a Russian-American track meet, the Russian coach was asked what he thought was his best strategy for training his fast young athletes.

Without a pause came the answer, "In the starting guns—we use *real* bullets!"

919.   After love, book collecting is the most exhilarating sport of all.

—*A. S. W. Rosenbach*

920.   At a college with a conference-leading football team, there was a first string wide receiver equally renowned for his spectacular catches and miserable grades. One day, the English professor asked him to name the main characters in *Romeo and Juliet*. The young man came up with this classic: "Sleepy, Dopey, Sneezy, Grumpy, Doc, and . . . I forget the rest . . ."

921.   It was the beginning of a beautiful spring weekend, and the teacher's wife decided to lay down the law immediately.

"Listen," she told him at breakfast, "don't think you're going to run off and play golf and leave me here with all the work."

"Golf is the furthest thing from my mind," the husband protested. "Now, will you please pass me the putter."

922. The teacher in a rural community school was reading to her class about the great swimmer Gertrude Ederle, the first woman to swim the English Channel.

"She swam the river behind her home three times every morning before breakfast just to get into training for her great feat," commented the teacher.

She was about to continue reading when several of the students began giggling.

"What are you laughing at?" she asked.

"Nothing, Ma'am," said one boy. "We're just wondering why she didn't make it *four* times and go back and get her clothes."

Statistics

923. A scientist quoting statistics should be reviewed with the same eye that the Bible cautions concerning the Devil quoting scriptures.

924. Statistics can prove anything. For instance, did you know that the French were the worst criminals in the world? After all, of all the crimes that take place in Paris, ninety-five per cent are committed by Frenchmen.

925. There are three types of falsehood—lies, damned lies, and statistics.

—Benjamin Disraeli

926. "How'd your apple crop do this year, Sam?"

"Dave, we had a terrible time. The worms got fifty per cent of it, and the rest was blown down by a freak wind storm."

"That's too bad, Sam. Could you use any of them?"

"Sure enough, Dave. I ate one, and you can have the other."

927. We hear so much about the statisticians who figure out the time people waste in every kind of work. Did they ever stop to figure out the time wasted figuring out the statistics?

928. "Sheila, would you marry a man just for his money?" asked the ardent young man

"Well," said Sheila, "it all depends on whether you're taking a survey or proposing."

Students

929. "I'd like to return this student lamp," said the young man to the department store clerk.

"I'm sorry, sir. Is it broken?"

"No, it works fine," said the student sadly, "but I flunked out."

930. Compare, anyone who can, the typical undergraduate (if he will sit still long enough to let you compare him) with the little schoolboy that once he was. Wither now has gone that wistful dawning intelligence. The clouds of glory that he trailed are blown by all the winds of the stadium. The child that wrote the verses for verses' sake, that saw visions in the pages of his books and heard in his ears the trampling feet and the armored horses of the past— wither has he vanished?

—*Stephen Leacock*

931. One young man was getting quite a reputation as the worst souse on campus. Finally, the Dean decided to have a talk with him. Calling the lad into his office, the Dean said bluntly, "Son, do you drink?"

"Well, sir," said the student, "it's a little early for me, but don't let me stop *you*."

932. Two fathers were talking about their college-student off-spring.

"Boy, my son is getting so smart, and his letters are so filled with big words, that I gotta use a dictionary to answer them."

"Count yourself lucky," said the other. "To answer my son's letters all I need is a checkbook."

933. Then there was the shy young coed who said she was going home because she was told that she would have to disrobe for gym.

As she explained to her mother, "I'm not getting undressed in front of any man, and I don't care what his name is!"

934. It used to be that a college kid was content to have just a picture of his girl in his room and dream—nowadays they've taken all the imagination out of it.

Study

935. There was one student who was always loafing around while his roommate was always at the books. Finally, the conscientious boy couldn't stand it any more.

"Aren't you ever going to study?" he asked.

"My friend," said the other student, "I look at it this way: The more I study, the more I know; the more I know, the more I forget; the more I forget, the less I know; the less I know, the less I forget; the less I forget, the more I know. Having thought all that out, I ask you, 'Why study?'"

936. "Oh, professor," said the coed as she wiggled her way into the educator's office, "I just want you to know that I would do anything to pass English—just anything!"

The professor looked her over as she sat and pulled up the hem of her already-brief skirt.

"Anything?" he asked.

"Anything," she cooed.

'Even study?"

937. The more we study, the more we discover our ignorance.

—Percy Bysshe Shelley

Substitute Teacher

938. Jane and Sally had been friends all through college. Jane, a teacher, was getting married, and Sally, a substitute teacher in the same system, offered to take over her friend's classes during the honeymoon.

At a party which Jane and her new husband held upon their return, someone offered to introduce the substitute teacher to the groom.

"Oh, I know Sally very well," smiled the groom. "She substituted for my wife on our honeymoon!"

939. "I asked God about you last night, Miss Jones."

"What did you ask, Johnny?"

"I asked Him to make sure you don't get sick."

"Why, Johnny, how nice . . ."

"Yeah, 'cause I always get in trouble when we have a substitute teacher."

940. Mrs. Amory had been a substitute in the system for many years and consequently had been in for each teacher several times.

One day she was called to take charge of a class of fifth graders. She looked and looked, but she could not find the teacher's Emergency Lesson Plans for that day's lessons.

"I'm so sorry," said the teacher upon her return.

"That's all right," said Mrs. Amory. "I found a couple of your plans from last year. I just changed the dates, added new names, and passed out your old dittos."

941. "Wow!" exclaimed little Tommy, "our substitute today was great. She only had *two* rules: Shut up! and Sit down!"

Success

942. Be satisfied with success in even the smallest matter, and think that even such a result is no trifle.

—Marcus Aurelius

943. "What's your name?" asked the prospective boss of the bright-eyed young man.

"Thomas Jefferson," replied the youth.

"That's a very famous name, you know," said the man.

"I know," replied the boy, "and that just shows you how good I was at pumping gas in my last job."

944. Nothing succeeds like success.

—Old French Proverb

945. In public we say the race is to the strongest; in private we know that a lopsided man runs the fastest along the little side-hills of success.

—Frank Moore Colby

946. If at first you don't succeed, you're running about average with other teachers.

947. A minute's success pays for the failure of years.

—Robert Browning

Summer

948.   When the glass is at ninety a man is a fool
        Who directs not his efforts to try to keep cool.

—Joseph Ashby-Sterry

949. The joyous summer chant of parents: "Pack off your troubles with their old camp bags and smile, smile, smile!"

950. Hasty note from camp: "Please send round cookies; all they serve here are square meals."

951.   Three-score summers, when they're gone,
             Will appear as short as one.

—*William Oldys*

Sunday School

952. When the Sunday School teacher related the biblical story of Abraham and Isaac, he became very dramatic. He described how poor Isaac was about to be sacrificed as Abraham lifted the dagger.

All at once, a little girl screamed from the tension.

"Be quiet, Betty," said an older child. "You know that in these stories God always comes in on the last page and rescues the guy!"

953. The Minister had just told the children the story of Daniel and the Lion's Den. When he had finished, he asked, "What does this story teach us?"

One little girl answered wide-eyed, "Not to go into strange, dark places without your Daddy."

954. "Mrs. James is a pillar of the church," the Minister remarked to his wife. "Why, do you know that she hasn't missed a single Sunday since the church was built, over fifty years ago?"

"Wow!" exclaimed their little son, "I bet God must sure be bored seeing the same old face every week!"

955. "You have to go to Sunday School, Dick," said the boy's father. "I went every Sunday when I was a boy."

"Gee, Dad," returned the son, "I bet it won't make me a better person either."

956. A Sunday School teacher asked a primary class where God lived. Expecting something like 'in heaven,' she was surprised when one little tyke said, "In our bathroom."

"What makes you say that, dear?"

"Because," she answered, "whenever my father goes there, he always knocks first and says, 'My God, are you still in there!' "

957. The pastor of the parish always asked the children the same questions, and in the same sequence: "What's your name? How old are you? Do you say your prayers? What will happen to you if you don't say your prayers?"

An overly ambitious mother had rehearsed her little boy with the answers, and when the pastor called on him the boy beat him to the punch by rattling off: "Billy Murry, six, yes, go to hell."

958. The question on the Sunday School test read, "Tell what you know about the Last Supper."

Answered one boy, "I had the measles and I couldn't attend, so I don't know what happened."

959. "How many of you would like to go to heaven?" asked the Sunday School teacher.

Everybody raised their hand except Jimmy.

"Why don't you want to go to heaven?"

"I do! I do!" cried Jimmy, "but we have to go to my grandmother's house for dinner right after church."

Superintendent

960. "When I was just out of college," said the wise Superintendent, "I thought it was my job to tell the people who worked *for* me what they were doing wrong. Now I find I can get a lot more done and do it better by telling the people who work *with* me what they're doing right.''

961. "Son," asked the Superintendent as he visited the high school history class, "who shot Lincoln?"

"Honest, Sir," stammered the youth, "I didn't do it."

Relating the story at the School Board meeting that night, it received the expected chuckles. The laugh-of-the-night honors, however, had to go to the Board member who snarled, "I bet you find out tomorrow that he really did do it!"

962. The Superintendent, a notoriously long-winded speaker, was asked to give the after-dinner speech. Rising from his chair, he began, "I think if I had eaten one more bite, I wouldn't have been able to deliver my speech tonight."

Just then there came a shout from the back of the room, "Somebody get that man another piece of cake!"

963. It doesn't take much to be a Superintendent these days—just a willingness to try the impossible, do without the indispensable, and endure the intolerable.

964. The Superintendent walked silently into his office and wasn't seen or heard from for several hours. Finally, his secretary gently knocked on his door and asked if anything was the matter.

"There sure is," sighed the man. "I got a look at the new aptitude tests we're going to be giving next week."

"Are they hard?" asked the puzzled woman.

"I didn't think so when I took mine," he replied, "but I just got back the results and found out that the smartest thing for me to do is to try to get an unskilled job."

965. The Superintendent was due for a visit, and the principal had stationed a boy in the hallway to watch out for his arrival. About five minutes after he had placed the lad, the principal returned and asked if the Superintendent had arrived. Receiving a negative answer, he was off, only to return a few minutes later with the same question.

Finally, the Superintendent did arrive, spotted the little boy, and asked, "Son, do you know who I am?"

"No, Sir," the boy replied.

"I am the Superintendent."

"Wow!" exclaimed the lad. "Are you in trouble! The principal's asked for you *twice* already!"

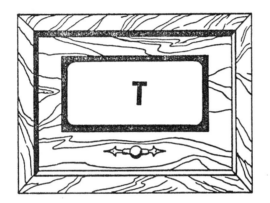

Tact

966. Mary was having dinner at her friend's house. When the meal was over, the friend's mother gave each child a slice of cake for dessert. When only crumbs were left, the mother asked Mary if she would like another helping.

"No, thank you," she said.

"Do have another," urged the friend's mother.

"My Mommy told me not to take second helpings," Mary explained, "but I'm sure she didn't realize how tiny the first helping would be."

967. You need more tact in the dangerous art of giving presents than in any other social action.

—William Bolitho

968.   Tact is the intelligence of the heart.

969.   It happened that one afternoon the principal found himself outside the school building. All the entry doors were locked, and he could not get back in.

Just then a third-grader came by, saw the situation, and let him in.

"Thank you, my lad," beamed the principal. "I'll have to speak to your class about your good deed."

"Excuse me, sir," interrupted the boy, "but if it's O.K. with you, can we keep this just between us. If the guys found out about it, they'd never forgive me."

970.   The art of being a gracious host is not to be bothered by late-staying guests; the mark of a gracious guest is to know when to leave. In this situation, as in life, tact is the buffer of misunderstanding.

971.   At a senior citizen's banquet, the college president was asked to give a talk on the advantage of returning to college. After the speech, he was approached by a perky little white-haired lady.

"I just had to talk to you," she said. "I think it's marvelous that your college has courses for old men and women."

"Thank you, Madam," said the president, "but people your age can join them, too."

972.   Never tell a woman that her face would stop a clock. Just tell her that when you look at her, time stands still.

Tardiness

973.   "Tommy," said the teacher, "you're ten minutes late again. Don't you know what time the class starts to work?"

"No, Miss Jones," answered Tommy. "They're always working already by the time I get here."

974. A man consumes the time you make him
Wait
In thinking of your faults—so don't be
Late!

—Arthur Guiterman

975. Better three hours too soon than a minute too late.

—William Shakespeare

Taxes

976. It is said that playing golf is like paying taxes—you drive hard to get to the green and then wind up in the hole.

977. When there is an income tax, the just man will pay more and the unjust less on the same amount of income.

—Plato

978. Congress should know how to levy taxes, and if it doesn't know how to collect them, then a man is a fool to pay them.

—J. P. Morgan

979. Walking along the street, a man was attracted by frightened screams coming from a house. Rushing in, he found the mother frantic because her small son had swallowed a coin. Seizing the child by the heels, he held him up, gave him a few quick shakes, and the coin dropped to the floor.

The grateful mother was loud in admiration.

"You certainly knew how to get it out of him," she said. "Are you a doctor?"

"No, Madam," the man replied, "I'm from the Internal Revenue Service."

980.   To tax the community for the advantage of a class is not protection; it is plunder.

—Benjamin Disraeli

981.   The class was writing a composition. One little boy, who wanted $100 very badly, wrote a personal letter to God, asking for it. His teacher, reading it, decided to try to get it for him by sending the request to the White House.

The President acknowledged the boy's request with a check for five dollars.

Delighted at having received at least a partial answer to his written prayer, the boy wrote a thank-you note to God.

"P.S." he added. "I see You routed the money through Washington, and they deducted their usual ninety-five per cent."

Teachers

982.   Those who educate children well are more to be honored than even their parents, for these only give them life; those the art of living well.

—Aristotle

983.   As a teacher I have taught a thief, a schizophrenic, an evangelist, and a murderer.

The thief was a tall boy who hid in the shadows and whom the other children avoided. The schizophrenic rarely spoke but gazed at me with tiny eyes filled with terror. The evangelist was class president and the most popular boy in school. The murderer sat and stared out the window, occasionally letting out a shriek that would shiver the glass.

The thief stands looking through the bars of his prison cell. In the state mental hospital the schizophrenic is restrained from beating his head on the floor. The evangelist sleeps in the church yard, victim of a disease contracted during his missionary work. The police no longer search for the murderer ever since he was, himself, killed in a bar-room brawl.

And all of them sat in my classroom and listened as I taught. I must have been a great help to them. After all, I taught them the difference between a noun and a verb, and how to diagram a sentence.

984. At a university with a medical school, the professors were somewhat chagrined to find an announcement on the wall of the faculty lounge urging that the educators leave their brains to science.

"All contributions," it read, "will be accepted, no matter how small."

985. Two ladies were sitting in a beauty parlor discussing a third who had just left.

"I don't care what she says," said one, "she is *not* a teacher. I never once heard her complain about the kids."

986. Could bribery really have started when the first child gave his teacher an apple?

987. I am not a teacher; only a fellow traveler of whom you asked the way. I pointed ahead—ahead of myself as well as of you.

—*George Bernard Shaw*

988. The good and the great teachers are that way because what they are as men is always a vital part of what they know as scholars. Theirs is the wisdom to realize that knowledge is no end in itself but desirable only as a means to enjoyment and life. If they teach well (in other words, if they are able to make the hard process of learning seem pleasant, exciting, and important to others) it is because they have so lived a subject that they can incite others to feel the need of adding it to their own living.

—*John Mason Brown*

Teaching

989.   The object of teaching a child is to enable him to get along without his teacher.

—*Elbert Hubbard*

990.   One of the main tasks of the school teacher is to take a roomful of live wires and see that they're grounded.

991.   The teacher was trying to get her class to stop contracting and shortening each other's names. She went around and asked each child to say his or her name.
"Theo," said one lad.
"No," corrected the teacher. "You mean Theo-*dore*."
She went on to the next child and asked his name.
"Steveadore," he replied.

992.   The one exclusive sign of thorough knowledge is the power of teaching.

—*Aristotle*

993.   At the commencement exercises of the local teacher's college, one new graduate who planned on getting married shortly was asked how long she intended to stay in the classroom.
Came her reply: "From here to maternity."

994.   Education is a thing of which only the few are capable; teach as you will, only a small percentage will profit by your most zealous energy.

—*George Gissing*

995. The class had spent most of the morning on their science reports. One little girl, not overly scientifically oriented, approached the teacher's desk.

"Mrs. Simon," she asked, "when are we going to have reading today?"

"Why, Mary," replied the teacher, "we've had reading, penmanship, science, and spelling all morning long as you did your reports."

"Wow!" exclaimed Mary. "You really fooled us. You were teaching us, and we didn't even know it."

996. In the education of children there is nothing like alluring the interest and affection; otherwise you only make so many asses laden with books.

—Michel de Montaigne

997. You must never tell a thing. You must illustrate it. We learn through the eye and not the noggin.

—Will Rogers

998.
A man knocked at the heavenly gate,
    His face was scarred and old.
He stood before the Man of Fate
    For admission to the fold.
"What have you done," St. Peter asked,
    "To gain admission here?"
"I've been a teacher, sir," he said,
    "For many and many a year."
The pearly gates swung open wide;
    St. Peter touched the bell.
"Come in and choose your harp," he said,
    "You've served your time in hell!"

Teen-agers

999. When my teen-age daughter leaves on a date,
      As pretty and sweet as a late summer bloom,
    I can always depend on this one simple rule:
      The clothes she once wore are all over her room.

1000. "My son and I get along fine," said one father of a teen-age boy. "He always does just what I tell him."

"That's really amazing," said his friend. "What do you do to make him so well behaved?"

"Actually, it's quite simple. I tell him to do what he wants."

1001. Teen-age fashion these days is proving the old adage, "The ends justify the jeans."

1002. The mother and her teen-age daughter were going at it again. The argument, too, was basically the same. The mother didn't like the way her daughter was wearing her hair, and the daughter was saying that *everybody* was doing it that way.

"I don't see why you all have to look like you're wearing mops!" exclaimed the mother.

"What's a mop?" asked the teen-ager.

And the fight was on again.

1003. The time had come. Tonight was her first big date. Going to the store, the teen-age girl gazed at all the perfumes on the counter. She looked and looked but didn't find what she wanted among "Embraceable," "Invitation," and "Come Hither." The saleslady, seeing her predicament, asked if she might be of help.

"I hope so," said the girl. "Do you have something like, 'Keep Your Distance?' "

Telephone

1004. The teacher was training his young son to answer the telephone. One afternoon he heard the phone ring. Several moments passed, and he called to his son.

"Who was that?" asked the father.

"I don't know, Dad. Some lady said it was long distance from California. I told her that we were studying that in school, and I knew it was. Then I hung up."

1005. Whenever you talk of the good old days, remember that the telephone was invented twenty-five years after the bathtub. This means that some lucky people got to soak for a quarter of a century without having to get out of the one to answer the other.

1006. "Oh, honey, look what I bought today," said the principal's wife as she showed him her new car.

"Alice, whatever possessed you to buy a car!"

"You see, dear," explained his wife, "I went in to use their telephone, and I hated to leave without buying something."

1007. The principal was at an educator's convention and decided to call home. Dialing the operator, he learned that it would cost him $1.25.

"Say, Miss," the man asked, "I'm calling my wife. Do you have a special rate for just listening?"

1008. The English professor was having trouble collecting his telephone messages from the college switchboard.

"This is Professor Whyte. No, not 'Wright.' Whyte—'W' as in Wordsworth, 'H' as in Hawthorne, 'Y' as in Yeats, 'T' as in Thackery, and 'E' as in Emerson—Whyte! Got it now?"

1009. The local telephone company was always getting strange requests, but the one they're still talking about came from an elderly lady. It seems that her telephone cord was too long, and she wanted the company to pull it back from their end.

Television

1010. If it weren't for T.V. commercials, no students would do their homework.

1011. "In our house," said the man, "I can always tell which T.V. shows are going to be cancelled even before it's reported."

"How's that?" asked his friend.

"I know a show is doomed when my kids leave it to do their homework."

1012. Two little tykes were glued to the T.V. set one Saturday morning. Before them were the exploits of "Captain Zero of the Planet Argon."

"Gee," sighed one, "I wish we hadn't been born in the past."

1013. "I bought a new T.V. yesterday," said the man, "and the first thing my wife and I saw on it was a movie which we had seen originally when we were just starting to court. At that time, as I recall, it cost me about 50 cents. Now, here's that same movie, and last night it cost me over four hundred dollars."

1014. The teacher took her fourth grade class to a museum. One of the rooms was a Roman living room exactly as it would have appeared in the time of Caesar.

"Can you see why times were rough back in those days?" asked the teacher.

"I sure can," volunteered one student. "They didn't have any T.V.!"

Theater

1015. The world's a stage, where God's omnipotence,
His justice, knowledge, love, and providence
Do act the parts.

—Guillaume de Salluste

1016. The prologue is the grace,
Each act, a course, each scene, a different dish.

—George Farquahr

1017. The mother had made a special trip to see her son appear in a play presented by the college dramatic society.

Arriving just in time, she hurried backstage to wish her son good luck.

"I do hope you're not frightened about appearing in front of an audience," commented the mother.

"Why should I be afraid?" asked her son. "The cast always outnumbers the audience anyway."

1018. One of my chief regrets from my years in the theater is that I couldn't sit in the audience and watch me.

—John Barrymore

Time

1019. "Don't you think it's time for a little son to be in bed?" father asked gently.

"I don't know, Daddy," said the lad, "but if you find out, be sure to tell me so I'll know when I have a son."

1020. "You apologize in one minute or I'll knock your block off!" said the little boy with his fists clenched.

"And if I don't in one minute?" said the other. "Watcha gonna do?"

"Err . . . ask you how much time you want?"

1021. The teacher had brought in an old clock for some of his students to work on in their spare time. The instrument was taken apart and put back together many times before one of the boys handed it to the teacher with the pronouncement that the clock was "better than new."

Just then the hour came around and the clock proceeded to strike fifty-seven times.

"See that!" exclaimed the boy. "That clock tells more time than I knew there could be."

1022. Time is the image of eternity.

—Plato

1023. The teacher was talking to her class about the amazing inventions produced in this century. She asked them what they thought was the greatest addition to America in the past twenty-five years.

"That's easy," smiled one boy. "Me!"

1024. We changed with the times, so we can't blame the kids for just joinin' the times without even havin' to change.

—Will Rogers

1025. "I must admit you're getting better," said mother. "You usually talk on the telephone for over an hour, but today you spoke less than twenty minutes. How come?"

"Wrong number," said the child.

1026.   Time on time revolving we decry,
                 So moments flit, so moments fly.

—Ovid

1027. Leave the dead moments to bury the dead.

—Owen Meredith

Tradition

1028. The tradition of all the dead generations weighs like a nightmare on the brain of the living.

—Karl Marx

1029. Have a place for everything and then keep the things someplace else; this isn't advice, it's just custom.

—Mark Twain

1030. Man must not check reason by tradition, but contrariwise, must check tradition by reason.

—Leo Tolstoy

Traits

1031. The college president was speaking at the commencement exercises.

"I must admit," he said, "that this class has given me so much trouble, that if the Lord had decided to take you all in one swoop, I wouldn't even have gone to the funerals.

"Now that you're graduating," he continued, "I am beginning to change my point of view. I'll be more than happy to go to any of your funerals—anytime."

1032. The basic trouble with kids today is that they are just as cantankerous, boisterous, lazy, and reckless as we were in our youth.

1033. If you can meet with Triumph and Disaster
And treat those two imposters just the same;
If you can talk with crowds and keep your virtue,
Or walk with Kings—nor lose the common touch . . .
Yours is the Earth and everything that's in it,
And—which is more—you'll be a Man, my son!

—Rudyard Kipling

Trips, Class

1034. En route to the Art Gallery, a cluster of boys surrounded one boy at the back of the bus. The teacher overheard the words of wisdom this lad was dispensing.

"Now, remember fellows, don't look at anything, 'cause she'll only make us write about it tomorrow!"

1035. The first-graders went on their traditional class trip to the dairy farm. Everything was going well until one little guy came running up to the teacher.

"Teacher! Teacher!" he exclaimed. "Come with me! Quick!"

Hurriedly the teacher followed the lad as he rounded the building and stood panting as he pointed to a pile of empty milk bottles.

"See!" he bubbled, "a cow's nest!"

1036. The class was taken to a bird sanctuary. They were fortunate enough to witness a flock of geese preparing to migrate. The birds squawked and fluttered.

"Billy," asked the teacher, "what do you think is going on? Why are they all so noisy?"

"If you ask me," said Billy, "the Daddy birds are screaming 'cause they're late, and the Mama birds are telling the kids to go to the bathroom."

1037.   The well-traveled may lie with impunity.

—*French Proverb*

Trust

1038.   Put not your trust in money, but put your money in trust.

—*Oliver Wendell Holmes*

1039.   Love, and do what you will.

—*St. Augustine*

1040.   When her brother made a snare to catch rabbits, his little sister announced that she thought that such a thing was terrible.

"You know what, Mommy?" she said. "Tonight I'm gonna pray real hard that the trap won't catch any rabbits. I know God will hear my prayers and won't let any bunnies be caught."

"It's a fine thing to have trust, dear," said her mother, "but I really think . . ."

"Besides," the girl interrupted in a whisper, "I went outside before and kicked it to pieces!"

1041.   The only way to make a man trustworthy is to trust him.

—*Henry Lewis Stimson*

1042.   The owner of the country store had to leave for a day to go to the big city. Calling the boy who worked for him, he pressed a key into the lad's hand.

"That's the key to the strongbox," he declared. "I want you to make sure that nobody goes near it while I'm away."

"You can trust me, sir," said the lad. "I'll make certain that no one comes within ten feet of it."

The merchant left and was waiting for the train at the station when he heard a commotion in the street. He rose just in time to see an automobile speed down the street, narrowly miss several pedestrians, and come to a screeching halt before the station. To his surprise, the man's youthful assistant tumbled out and ran up to him.

"Thank goodness I caught you before the train left!" the boy exclaimed. "You left the wrong key!"

1043. The battle of the sexes was going full tilt between the boy and the girl.

"Women," he proclaimed, "cannot be trusted too far!"

"And men," the girl rejoined, "can't be trusted too near!"

Truth

1044. Even a liar tells a hundred truths to one lie; he has to, to make the lie good for anything.

—Henry Ward Beecher

1045. The most truthful letter of resignation ever received came from the school teacher who was requesting maternity leave.

"Dear Sir," the letter ran, "I am getting too big for this job . . ."

1046. "Mommy!" exclaimed the child as she rushed into the house, "we stopped on the way home from school for a treat."

"That's nice, dear," said mother. "What did Daddy get you?"

"I had a soda," she answered, "but all Daddy had was a glass of water with an olive in it."

1047.   The highest compact we can make with our fellow is,— "Let there be truth between us two forever more."

—*Ralph Waldo Emerson*

1048.   Poets are all who love, who feel great truths,
And tell them; and the truth of truths is love.

—*Philip James Bailey*

1049.   The teacher read her husband's fortune from the penny weight scale.

"It says that you are dynamic," she read, "a natural leader, and are strong of character. Hmmm, it got your weight wrong, too."

1050.   Cannon-balls may aid the truth,
But thought's a weapon stronger;
We'll win our battles by its aid;—
Wait a little longer.

—*Charles Mackay*

1051.   The little girl was kneeling beside her bed saying her night-time prayers. Mother strained her ears as the child mumbled into folded hands.

"Excuse me, dear," mother interrupted, "but could you speak a little clearer. I really can't hear you."

"That's all right, Mommy," said the little girl, "I wasn't talking to you."

1052.   The untruthful man's punishment is not in the least that he is not believed, but that he cannot believe anyone else.

—*George Bernard Shaw*

1053.   One of the teachers was an avid fisherman, and he always bragged of the "big ones" that he caught on weekends and vacations. The only trouble was that the rest of the faculty viewed his boasts with a somewhat jaundiced eye.

"I'll prove it," he said, and the next Monday morning the teacher brought in his catch of the weekend and a fish scale. In the presence of all, he dutifully weighed the fish and vindicated himself.

Later that day, the science teacher borrowed the fish scale for an experiment in class.

"That was the first time in my entire career," the science teacher reported, "that a spoonful of salt weighed thirty-two pounds!"

Underachievers

1054.   He rarely Hits the Mark or Wins the Game
Who says, "I Know I'll Miss!"
While taking Aim.

—*Arthur Guiterman*

1055.   The student walked in rather early from his date, and his roommate was curious.

"I thought that girl you met had invited you up to her apartment," he said.

"She did," answered the other.

"But it's only ten o'clock."

"I know," the student said with a frown. "We were getting along just fine, and then she excuses herself. When she comes out, she's in a negligee and the first thing she does is turn down the lights. Well, I figured if she was getting ready to go to sleep, that was my hint to get going."

1056.   The two first-graders were seated on a bench in the principal's office.

"Hi," said one of them to the other. "I'm an underachiever; what's your racket?"

1057.   The most gladsome thing in the world is that few of us fall very low; the saddest that, with such capabilities, we seldom rise high.

—Sir James M. Barrie

1058.   "Class," said the teacher, "we have a real treat today. A man from the local zoo is coming to put on a show about animals."

"How much is it gonna cost to see it?" asked one boy.

"It's free to all students," replied the teacher.

"I'll bet it's after school," continued the lad.

"No, it takes place during school time."

"How long is it gonna be?"

"The show will last an hour."

"I knew it!" exclaimed the little boy. "I knew there had to be a catch—my attention span is only twenty-five minutes!"

1059.   God knows, I'm not the thing I should be,
            Nor am I even the thing I could be.

—Robert Burns

1060.   Oh, the little more, and how much it is!
            And the little less, and what worlds away!

—Robert Browning

Understanding

1061.   There are those who understand everything until someone puts it into words.

—Francis Bradley

1062.   It's man's mission to learn to understand.

—Vannevar Bush

1063.   The body travels more easily than the mind; until we have limbered up our imaginations we continue to think as though we had stayed at home. We really have not budged a step until we have taken up residence in someone else's point of view.

—John Erskine

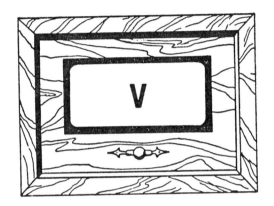

Vacations

1064. When the teacher announced that she would be getting married over the summer vacation period, both faculty and students were quick to offer congratulations. One teacher had her class of second-graders write little notes of congratulations which they delivered to the soon-to-be-bride.

The note that made the rounds of the teacher's room came from one little girl who wrote, "Have a good vacation and a sexfull married life."

1065. The bigger the summer vacation, the harder the fall.

1066. When the overwrought teacher went to the doctor for her nerves, the man prescribed a vacation. She claimed that she was too busy to take time off.

"Why," she went on, "I work like those marvelous ants—never stopping, never stopping."

"That may be," replied the medical man, "but even they find time to attend picnics."

1067. The teacher had saved for years for the trip, and her vacation money was carefully budgeted.

One day on her tour of the Holy Land, she wanted to take a boat trip on the Sea of Galilee. The price was over ten dollars in American money. She complained to the guide that that was too high.

"But, Madam," said the guide, "the Lord walked on that water."

"The Lord was a teacher," she replied stiffly. "Of course He walked; He was probably on a budget, too!"

1068. When the young teacher returned to school after summer vacation, she met an older teacher in the hallway.

"How was your summer vacation?" the older teacher asked.

"Wonderful," said the younger, "I met this man . . ."

"My dear," the other teacher interrupted, "you should know better than to trust these summer romances. Take it from me, they never come to anything."

"Are you sure of that?"

"Quite sure."

"In that case," the younger teacher said as she held up her left hand and wiggled her gold-banded finger, "make certain you don't tell my new husband."

1069. During her vacation the teacher went for a ride through Rome. Coming upon the tumbled ruins of an ancient temple, she stopped to take a closer look. One of the locals asked her if she would like to have her picture taken against the ruins to show the folks back home.

"That would be nice," she said, "but please don't get the car in the picture or my husband will think I knocked it down."

1070. "Mom! Pop!" exclaimed the boy as he tumbled off the bus from summer camp. "I won an award in camp! I had the neatest suitcase!"

"Amazing." smiled mother. "Those three weeks at camp must have done you some good. We could never get you to be neat at home, and now you have the neatest trunk in camp. How did you do it?"

"Simple," the youth beamed. "After you got me ready to go to camp, I just never unpacked."

1071. Ask any teacher, and he'll tell you that summer vacation is a time which makes you feel good enough to go back to work and poor enough to have to.

Values

1072. When a man falls in love with himself, he's usually starting a life-long romance.

1073. Even bees know there is rich juice in poison flowers.

—John Keats

1074. Fools rush in where angels fear to tread.

—Alexander Pope

1075. The story was told that when Western Union offered to buy the ticker invented by Thomas Edison, the great inventor was unable to set a price. He asked for a couple of days to consider. Talking the matter over with his wife, she suggested he ask twenty thousand dollars, but Edison thought this was exorbitant. At the appointed time, Edison presented himself at the Western Union office. He was asked to name a price. Edison tried to say twenty thousand dollars, but lacked the courage and just stood there speechless.

The official waited a minute, then broke the silence by saying, "Well, how do you feel about one hundred thousand dollars?"

Vice-Principal

1076. The vice-principal was observing classes. One teacher bragged that she had taught the class how to observe with all their senses, and she asked if he would care to test them.

"Certainly," said the vice-principal. Then, turning to the class he said, "All right, children, close your eyes."

They did, and the man made a small chirping sound.

"Now," he said, "what did I do while your eyes were closed?"

"I know," said one lad. "You kissed the teacher!"

1077. The woman who lived adjacent to the school came storming into the office of the vice-principal.

"I want to know what you're going to do about it," she demanded.

"Do about what?" he asked.

"Some children from this school wrote dirty words on my fence, but that's not the worst part."

"Oh?"

"Yes," continued the woman. "They didn't even spell them correctly."

1078. The energetic, new vice-principal spent his first days in his new position putting signs all over the school. They read, "Do it now!" and "Don't put off until tomorrow what you can do today!" and "Don't Hesitate—Do it!"

A month into the school year, the superintendent chanced to meet the vice-principal on the street, and he asked how the poster campaign was going.

"It's too early to tell for sure," said the vice-principal, "but so far the drop-out rate has increased, four teachers have asked for maternity leave, and the football coach ran off with my secretary!"

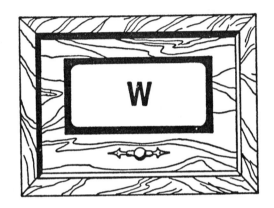

Weight

1079. "I'm so sad," said the teacher to her friend as they sat in the teacher's room one day. "My husband bought me a beautiful birthday present, and I can't fit into it."

"There, there," consoled her companion. "I know of a reducing salon right here in town. They'll get you into that dress in no time."

"What dress?" replied the other. "I'm talking about a Volkswagen!"

1080. According to one teacher we know who is a perpetual dieter, the best way to lose weight quickly is to eat all that you want of every food that you can't stand.

1081. "I went to my doctor last week about my weight problem," said the principal, "and he gave me some wonderful diet pills. Why, it's been less than a week, and already I've lost four pounds."

"That is marvelous," remarked a colleague. "I suppose you take one before each meal?"

"Oh, I don't take any," replied the principal.

"But if you don't take them, how . . ."

"I do exactly what my doctor suggested," the principal stated. "Three times a day I spill the entire bottle of pills on the floor and pick them up, one at a time!"

1082. A really busy person never knows how much he weighs.

—*Edgar Watson Howe*

1083. "I'm going to lose so much weight that you won't recognize me," the teacher told her colleagues one day. "I got this absolutely fantastic diet."

"What's it like?" asked another teacher.

"It's tremendous," stated the first. "You drink nothing but malted milks, you eat a gallon of ice cream each day, you have double helpings of potatoes, rich sauces, and bread and butter, and you snack three times between every meal."

"Goodness!" exclaimed her friend. "With that diet you'll weigh a ton in no time at all!"

"That's the secret," the first teacher whispered conspiratorially. "Nobody sticks to a diet."

1084.   And why I'm so plump the reason I'll tell,—
        Who leads a good life is sure to live well.

—*John O'Keeffe*

1085. As thin as the home made soup that was made by boiling the shadow of a pigeon that had been starved to death.

—*Abraham Lincoln*

Wisdom

1086.   One wise man's verdict outweighs all the fools'.

—*Robert Browning*

1087.   The wisdom that comes with age usually comes too late to do any good.

1088.
There never was a lion
Took more than he could eat,
Or a tired hippopotamus
Who didn't lie down to sleep.
No kangaroo has ulcers
That give severe attacks;
No canine ever worried
About his income tax.
Then *we*, with wisdom our intent,
The term "Dumb Animals" invent,
And go call *Man* "intelligent"?

1089.   The college student had taken a summer job waiting tables in a fashionable cocktail lounge. At one of his tables a patron, obviously having consumed somewhat above his limit, had passed out.

"Hadn't you better get him out of there?" suggested one of the other waiters. "You won't make any tips that way."

"Look, pal," said the college boy, "I'm no fool. Every time I wake him up, he pays the bill and throws in a generous tip!"

1090.   Life is a tragedy for those who feel, and a comedy for those who think.

—*Jean de LaBruyere*

1091.   It is the wisdom of crocodiles, to shed tears when they would devour.

—Francis Bacon

1092.   "Billy," said the teacher, "Why are you scratching yourself like that?"

"I have to, teacher," came his reply. "No one else knows where I itch."

1093.   Vice is a monster so frightful of mein
                   As to be hated needs but to be seen;
                   Yet seen too oft, familiar with her face,
                   We first endure, then pity, then embrace.

—Alexander Pope

1094.   A wise man sees as much as he ought, not as much as he can.

—Michel de Montaigne

1095.   It is always safe to learn, even from our enemies; seldom to instruct, even our friends.

—C. C. Colton

1096.   Happiness is not having what you want, but wanting what you have.

—Hyman Judah Schachtel

1097.   The teacher in the rural community was instructing her class in antonyms.

"What is the opposite of 'new'?" she asked one child.

" 'Old,' " the child answered.

"What is the antonym of 'down'?" she asked another.
" 'Up.' "
"And Tommy, what is the opposite of 'woe'?"
Answered the farm boy, " 'Giddy-up'!"

Words

1098. 'Verbosity' may be defined as the use by anyone in general or no one in particular of an excess in verbiage to communicate and otherwise get across to the listener or reader an idea or thought or some such image or bit of knowledge whether real or imagined that might have been said with a great deal more compactness and impact if proffered to the person with whom one was communicating in a simple and forthright manner without the use of so many unnecessary words.

1099.   But words are things, and a small drop of ink,
          Falling like dew upon a thought, produces
          That which makes thousands, perhaps millions, think.

                                        —Lord Byron

1100.   They that are rich in words, must needs discover
          That they are poor in that which makes a lover.

                                        —John Donne

1101. That teachers must teach connotation and shades of meaning was brought home by the ninth-grader who had, as a vocabulary word, the word "tawdry."

Looking it up in the dictionary, the youth found it defined as "cheap and tasteless."

The teacher found the word used in this sentence: "The cafeteria serves tawdry sandwiches."

1102.   Three things never come again. . . .
                   Never to the bow that bends
                   Comes the arrow that it sends. . . .
                   Never comes the chance that passed,
                   That one moment was its last. . . .
                   Never shall thy spoken word
                   Be again unsaid, unheard.

—Rose Terry Cooke

1103. "What are you writing?" asked the college student's roommate.

"It's my paper for my biology course," replied the writer. "I call it, *An Examination of the Profusion of Musculature in Interaction with Significant Psychological and Physiological Phenomena Which Produce Self-Inspired Ambulation.*"

"What?" asked the roommate.

"How People Walk," answered the other.

1104. Speech is civilization itself. The word, even the most contradictory word, preserves contact—it is silence which isolates.

—Thomas Mann

Worry

1105. Worry, the interest paid by those who borrow trouble.

—George Washington Lyon

1106. "I only worry about two things," said the teacher to her friend. "One of them is that I'm not doing something right, and that's why I have discipline problems, and the other is that I am doing everything right, and I still have discipline problems."

1107. "What's the matter, Tom?" asked the principal. "You're usually the most cheerful teacher in school, but lately you've been looking worried."

"I know," said the teacher. "It's just that I was so happy, I began to worry that I was too optimistic."

1108. Billy was normally the first child out the door at the end of the school day.

One day, his teacher noticed him purposely dawdling as he straightened his desk, put his books away, and began to pick up scraps around his desk area.

"Billy, is there something wrong?" his teacher finally asked.

"Yes, Ma'am," replied Billy, "I'm afraid to go home."

"Did you do something wrong?"

"Oh, no Ma'am. You see, Mom lost her book on how to raise children, and she's been using her own judgment ever since!"

1109. There are two days in the week about which and upon which I never worry. One of these days is Yesterday and the other is Tomorrow.

—*Robert Jones Burdette*

Writing

1110. It was reported that the great American author Sinclair Lewis was once asked to give a lecture on writing to a group of college students.

"Looking out at this gathering," he said to the assembled students, "makes me want to know how many of you *really and truly* wish to become writers."

Every hand in the room went up. Lewis looked at them for a moment, and then folded his notes and put them away.

"If that's true," he said, "then the best advice I can give you is to go home and write."

And he left the room.

1111.   When you've got a thing to say,
        Say it! Don't take half a day . . .
        Life is short—a fleeting vapor—
        Don't you fill the whole blamed paper
        With a tale which, at a pinch,
        Could be cornered in an inch!
        Boil her down until she simmers,
        Polish her until she glimmers.

—Joel Chandler Harris

1112.   "Mary, this essay on your cat bears a striking resemblance to the one your sister turned in last year."

"Yes, Ma'am," replied Mary, "it should; it's the same cat."

1113.   "Let us suppose," the creative writing teacher told his class, "that your hero wants to ask his girl's father for permission to marry her. You wouldn't have him say anything trite, but just how many ways can you have him ask the old man? Can any of you think of something?"

"You could always have him go up to the old boy," answered one of the brighter students, "and say, 'Sir, have I come up with an absolutely marvelous way for you to save a great deal of money!' "

1114.   The next time you start envying the kids the "carefree joys" of college, remember the midnight writing of term papers, theses, compositions, and job applications. You see, all those kids really have is writer's cramp!

1115.   The teacher asked her third-grade students to write a short paragraph on "Soap."

Wrote one little boy, "Soap is a large white thing that gets smaller and dirtier the more you rub it."

1116.   Writing, when properly managed (as you may be sure I think mine is) is but a different name for conversation.

—Laurence Sterne

1117. "Jimmy," said the teacher, "your composition on milk was supposed to be two pages long, but this is only half a page. What happened?"

"Don't tell me," said Jimmy, "that you've never heard of evaporated milk?"

1118.   Give me a condor's quill! Give me Vesuvius' crater for an inkstand! To produce a mighty book you must choose a mighty theme.

—Herman Melville

'X,' The Letter

1119. "Our alphabet is stupid," declared the boy. "Look at the letter 'X,' for instance. What good is it? We hardly ever use it."

"We need it!" exclaimed his little sister. "How else could we send kisses through the mail?"

1120. "Mommy! Mommy!" shouted Jimmy as he ran in after school, "my teacher loves me!"

"How do you know that?" asked his mother.

"She sent me kisses," he replied. "Just look at these x's all over my spelling paper."

1121. The algebra teacher was concluding the proof on the blackboard.

"So we see," he stated, "that X is equal to zero."

"You mean," exclaimed one student, "that we went through all this work for nothing!"

1122. The teacher had gone through Roman numerals with her class. Now she wrote "LXXX" on the blackboard.

"Jane," she said, peering at one child who, the teacher was certain, had not paid attention, "what does that stand for?"

Without hesitation the child responded, "Love and kisses?"

1123. "Have a Merry Xmas," wrote the teacher on the blackboard.

To which, one little boy added, "—all you Xians!"

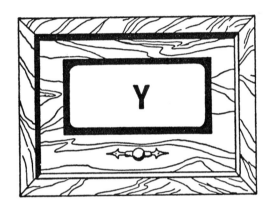

Youth

1124. Youth is a wonderful thing. What a crime to waste it on children.

—George Bernard Shaw

1125. The child's aunt had come for a visit.

After they had played for a while, the aunt remarked, "Oh, how I would like to know what it feels like to be a child!"

"I can fix that, Aunt Mary," replied the child. "I'll get Mommy to spank you."

1126. The octogenarian professor was walking across the campus with a colleague when he spied a shapely coed and let out a long wolf whistle.

"George," admonished his friend, "surely you are old enough to be beyond that sort of thing."

"You're right," the elderly professor replied sadly. "It's just that sometimes I get to feeling like I'm seventy again."

1127. Young men want to be faithful and are not;
Old men want to be faithless and cannot.

—Oscar Wilde

1128. The energy of youth increases in direct proportion to the fatigue of the parents.

1129. On the day your child is born, begin to teach him to do without things. The children of today are too much in love with luxury. They have execrable manners, flaunt authority, and have no respect for their elders. They no longer rise when their parents or teachers enter the room. I can only fear what kind of awful creatures they will be when they grow up.

—Socrates, 399 B.C.

1130. In sorrow he learned this truth—
One may return to the place of his birth,
He cannot go back to his youth.

—John Burroughs

1131. Any parents who attempt to clean up their children's rooms are probably the type of people who go out to shovel the walk *during* the snowstorm.

1132. Youth is the best time to be rich; and the best time to be poor.

—Euripides

1133. Young men are apt to think themselves wise enough, as drunken men are apt to think themselves sober enough.

—*Lord Chesterfield*

1134.   Youth should heed the older-witted
          When they say, don't go too far—
          Now their sins are all committed,
          Lord, how virtuous they are!

—*Wilhelm Busch*

Zoo

1135. Mama Gorilla took her son aside and pointed to the group of hooting, wildly-gesticulating school children who gathered around the cage hooting and hollering and jumping up and down.

"Don't be frightened, Junior," explained Mama Gorilla. "The bars are there to keep them out!"

1136. "Are you going to take me to the zoo?" asked the rambunctious child.

"No, dear," answered his harried mother. "If they want you, they'll just have to come and get you."

1137. The tour guide was showing the school children through the zoo when he stopped in front of the kangaroo cage.

"Here," he explained, "we have a native of Australia . . ."

"Good grief!" exclaimed little Tommy. "No wonder my father was upset; my sister married one of those!"

And Always Remember . . .

Laugh, and the world
   laughs with you;
Weep, and you weep
   alone;
For the sad old earth must
   borrow its mirth,
But has trouble enough
   of its own.

—*Ella Wheeler Wilcox*

Part II

What Do You Do If . . .

A Troubleshooter's Handy Guide to Every Speaking Occasion

Everyone has problems, and the public speaker is certainly no exception. The speaker's problems, however, are unique, because they are shared, willingly or unwillingly, by the people he addresses. The old maxim that, "If anything can go wrong, it will!" seems particularly appropriate when applied to speaking before an audience.

The siren that goes off in the middle of your speech, the member of the audience who asks you an obviously hostile question, the audience that is tired and restless before you rise to speak—all these and more prove a fantastic challenge for the speaker. It is, fortunately, a challenge that may be met and overcome.

Over the years, we have acquired a number of techniques for successfully dealing with those gremlins which beset the speaker. Some we acquired through sheer admiration for their simplicity and effectiveness, while others were developed out of an abiding need for self-preservation. All, however, have been audience-tested and successfully handled the problem to which they are addressed. We would like to share them with you.

On the following pages we have placed a series of problems which complete the question, "What do you do if . . ." Following each is the answer we have found to be the most effective. It is our sincere hope that they will serve you as well as they have worked for us.

With that in mind, let's take a look at some of the most common problems faced by speakers as we ask ourselves:

What Do You Do If . . .

. . . You Do Not Feel Well . . .

If you are seriously ill, of course, you will cancel your appearance, but we are not speaking of that type of illness here. What we are concerned with is the common cold, the end stages of a virus, the cough—those annoyances which, while they don't keep us confined to a sick bed, nevertheless may affect our speaking by providing self-made interruptions in the form of sneezes, coughs, and the necessity of nose-blowing. If all this sounds funny, let us assure you that it is anything but funny if you are the speaker so afflicted.

We have found that the most successful approach is to acknowledge the fact of your illness before you begin to speak, then forget about it, give your speech, and acknowledge the illness once more at the closing.

For example, you rise to speak, look at your audience, and say, "Ladies and Gentlemen, I have a cold. It's not serious, but if you should hear my speech interrupted by a loud sneeze, it will most likely be me. I hope you will bear with me, and we'll get through it together." Then, you give your speech exactly as you have prepared it. Should you have to sneeze or accommodate stuffy sinuses, you don't fight it—just do it as naturally and quickly as you can. Since you have already informed the audience of your malady, you need not keep constantly apologizing, but can concentrate on delivering your speech as effectively as possible. Finally, when you are finished, you will probably want to insert a short thank-you for their indulgence.

Not only have you effectively handled your illness, but your audience as well.

... You Have to Fill In ...

It goes something like this: You've just introduced the main speaker. "Ladies and Gentlemen, I give you Mr. Jones." Only there is no Mr. Jones. Perhaps he is out in the hallway putting his slides in order or any one of a dozen other places—but he is not there. Someone whispers, "I'll get him. Just keep talking!"

That is, of course, just one example of the instances where you have to "fill in" when something goes wrong. There are many more. The problem, however, is the same whatever occasioned it: You must fill in the time until normal procedures can be resumed.

Your answer is equally universal: Be honest—tell the audience what has happened and make it appear as an opportunity in disguise. Let's look at an example of just such an incident.

"Ladies and Gentlemen, there is going to be a short delay. I didn't realize that Mr. Jones had stepped away from the table, but he'll be back shortly, and I know we're going to enjoy his presentation. However, I'm really rather grateful to have these moments with you, for I'm certain you would like to help me express appreciation to the fine people who arranged this dinner tonight."

Thereafter, you can comment as long as is necessary about the hard work that goes into a dinner, the fine job the committee did, and you can introduce each person on the committee and lead individual applause for each one. When you spot your friend returning with Mr. Jones in tow, you can quickly close with something like, "Let's hear it one more time for the committee! And now, here he is—in the flesh this time—Mr. Jones!"

... You Want to Answer Questions in the Best Possible Manner ...

One of the severest tests of a good speaker is the ability to answer questions from the floor in a tight, efficient and effective manner. All else aside, if a question from the floor is handled in a halting, stammering, erratic manner, may not the audience begin to suppose that the speaker is either unsure of his material or trying to mislead them in some way?

Fortunately, there is a way, a tested and proven way, of answering questions that not only conveys to the audience exactly the information which their question requires, but does so in such a precise and effective manner that both the answer and the answerer are remembered.

The method involves two steps. When asked a question from the floor:

1. Repeat the question.
2. Use the A*R*E*A formula of response.

Let's examine each of these steps.

When you are asked a question from the floor, the first thing you ought to do is to repeat the question. This serves two purposes. First, it insures that everyone has heard the question and heard it exactly as the questioner intended. Second, it gives you time to think.

Quite often, the only one to hear the question is the speaker and the few people in the immediate vicinity of the questioner. This may be due to the acoustics of the hall or the soft-spoken manner of the questioner, but it happens more often than not. Therefore, your repetition of the question gives the rest of the audience the chance to hear what has been said. It also insures that what you have heard is what the questioner indeed asked, so there will be no confusion later or claims that the question was not answered.

Repeating the question also provides you with time to think and organize your answer. You will be surprised at how even a few seconds provides you time to get your material into order for presentation.

When it comes to actually answering the question that has been asked, there is no better or effective way of presenting your viewpoint than the use of the A*R*E*A formula. Each letter stands for one step in an effective answer. They are:

A—Answer
R—Reason

E—Example
A—Answer

First, give your *answer*. Make the point you wish to make. Tell the questioner the answer, the reason, the point that his question engenders.

Next, tell the *reason* for your answer. Tell clearly and concisely *why* you gave the answer you did.

Third, give an *example* that shows why you gave the answer you did. There is nothing like a concrete example to get across a salient point. Almost anything can be put into the form of an anecdote or story to which an audience can relate, no matter how intelligent you may think them to be. *Everyone* profits from a solid example.

Finally, repeat your *answer*. This time it should be a natural outgrowth of your reason and example. Also, leaving the questioner and, by projection, the audience with the answer gives them something to think about and something which they will remember for some time.

Now let's look at how the whole method would be used in an actual situation. Suppose you were speaking, and it came time for questions. The person you call upon rises and asks, "Why do you feel that heterogeneously grouped classes are better than homogeneously grouped ones?"

"The question has been asked," you state to the audience, "why I feel that heterogeneously grouped classes are better than homogeneously grouped classes. Is that correct? It is. I assume you mean 'better for students involved,' is that correct? It is. Thank you."

You have been addressing the questioner. You now turn and give your answer to the audience as a whole.

"I personally feel that heterogeneously grouped classes are better for students than homogeneously grouped classes because they allow for more flexibility in teaching methods and greater student-initiated help and aid. When a teacher uses a variety of methods, as she must in a heterogeneously grouped classroom, *all* children benefit because the material is covered from several different angles. Furthermore, the students who get the material more slowly can benefit from the aid of those children who get it more quickly, while at the same time reinforcing that knowledge in the quicker learning child. For example, let's take a math problem—five times three equals fifteen. For some, just the explanation of the mechanics and techniques of multiplication is enough, but in a heterogeneously grouped classroom, a teacher might also use three sets of five students walking to the front of the room. She might also let students come up with their own examples which they would 'share' with others, thereby insuring their learning and the others' learning as well. Everyone participates and grows from the interaction. Therefore, I feel that heterogeneously grouped classes are much more beneficial in education.''

Notice how, in this example, the question was not only repeated but a potential area of misunderstanding was clarified before it caused any concern. Then notice how the question was answered in strict accord with the A*R*E*A formula. Notice, too, that the entire thing was concise and did not ramble.

The next time you watch a televised press conference with any politico, pay attention to how he or she handles the questions asked by reporters. You will see them repeating questions, and if you pay particular attention, you just might see the A*R*E*A formula looking back at you from the television screen.

While a huge factor in an audience's acceptance of an answer is the personality of the speaker, still, a decided factor is the way in which the answer has been presented to them. Repeat that question, then give your answer, give the reason for your answer, give a good, solid example, and then repeat your answer, and you will have answered that question with effectiveness and dispatch.

... You Are Asked an Inane Question ...

It happens frequently. You have just finished speaking, and someone asks you a question which you have covered in your speech not five minutes before. Or, someone asks you a question that is akin to the ludicrous. For example, someone may ask, ''Is it true that the teachers in this school make sixty-thousand dollars a year each?'' What do you do if you are faced with questions equally as inane or misinformed or about material which you have just covered in your speaking?

What you never do, under any circumstances, is to make light of the question or the questioner. The audience may titter or even moan, but for you, the speaker, to ''put down'' the questioner or to laugh at or ridicule the question itself, will alienate your audience forever. If you have ''made fun'' of *one* of them, then you probably have contempt for *all* of them—or at least so the reasoning seems to go. The resultant veiled antagonism will negate any good you have accomplished up to this point and may erect a wall barring any future communication.

Tread lightly. Make no attempt at humor and avoid anything that even smacks of sarcasm, but answer the question in as serious and straight-forward a manner as possible. Be gentle and understanding with the questioner but not condescending. State your point of view and make every effort to see to it that your questioner is satisfied with the answer.

If, for example, you had been asked the question about teacher's salaries which was mentioned above, you would avoid all impulses to label it as an inane question even if the audience were roaring with laughter. You would answer that teacher's salaries are a matter of public record, that what he had asked was not the truth, and that he was more than welcome to examine any records he needed to satisfy himself as to the truth.

You will find that the audience will applaud not only your answer, but you as an understanding and concerned person as well.

... You Are Interrupted by a Loud Noise ...

In the middle of your speech the fire siren goes off with a piercing howl, a waiter drops a tray full of dishes, a dramatic thunderstorm splits the skies—these are just a few of the possible ''noise'' interruptions which may face the speaker. Whatever the cause, it is something which must be handled.

One school of thought claims that you merely ignore the interruption and continue. We don't agree. If the interruption was loud enough to get through to you, then it has gotten through to the audience as well. You may ignore it—but they won't.

Your answer lies in the way your audience reacts to the incident. When you are interrupted, the audience becomes unsettled, and they look to you to see how *you* are affected by it. If you accept it graciously, so will they, for in the majority of cases the audience wants to see you succeed.

Therefore, remember that being prepared is half the battle. Think of some interruptions that could occur, and prepare a word or two about them which you can deliver "spontaneously" upon their occurrence. After all, every speaker knows that the best "ad libs" are those which have been prepared in advance.

Whatever you say, make certain that you say it with a wide smile. This tells your audience that everything is all right; these things happen; let's have a good laugh about it and then get back to the business at hand.

Once, a colleague was speaking when there occurred a loud clap of thunder which rattled the windowpanes. The speaker paused, looked directly at the ceiling with arms spread and palms upturned, and said, "Did I say something You didn't like?"

The laughter drowned out the thunder.

... You Are Faced with a Hostile Audience ...

This is not a far-fetched assumption, particularly for the educator who may find himself addressing groups of citizens suspicious of "new" programs and weary of tax increases. There may, indeed, come a time when you, as a speaker, must face an audience that is not willing and eager to accept what you have to say; that may, in fact, be hostile.

It will not be easy, but it can be made bearable and antagonism can be kept to a minimum if you keep a few rules in mind:

1. Acknowledge, in the beginning, the fact that there are differences of opinion: "You may not agree with what I have to say tonight . . ."

2. Do not apologize for yourself: ". . . but I believe in what I am about to tell you, and all I ask is that you hear me out . . ."

3. Base what you say on hard, cold *facts*: ". . . As I see it, *these* are the facts of the matter . . ."

4. *Never* get personal: To attack their personal beliefs or opinions is your surest avenue to complete alienation. Let the weight of your argument win them to your side.

5. Be aware of the possibility of hostile questions: Handle these questions with tact and by stating provable facts, never opinions.

Under any circumstances, facing a hostile audience is a far from pleasant experience. Fortunately, 99% of your public speaking will be before receptive audiences, but it is well to be prepared for the unpleasant possibility. In such cases, you will survive if you follow the rules above and make every effort to project an image of confidence, assuredness, and calm.

. . . You Are Faced with an Argumentative Member of the Audience . . .

It doesn't happen often, but when it does, the speaker had better be prepared to handle it. This particular member of the audience may be defined as that person who *will not let you continue.* Not that you will have someone "heckle" you—as an educator you will not be addressing that type of audience—but you may have someone ask you a question, hostile or otherwise, and then refuse to let the matter drop. Perhaps he will press a point he particularly espouses or perhaps he will argue with some point in your answer to his original question, but he will not stop, and he will not allow you to continue.

The key to handling this problem effectively is to get the audience on your side while handling the hostile member with tact and understanding. No attempt should be made to belittle, make fun of, or put down the person so involved, even if the audience is obviously unhappy with him. In fact, the calmer you are and the more annoyed the audience becomes with the hostile member, the better it becomes for you.

Begin by answering all of his questions in a civil manner. Make certain you add, "Does that answer your question?" at the end of each answer. As long as he continues to ask questions, you should answer them. When, however, he begins to make a speech, you should not play along with his game. Remember that you are there to answer questions; not engage in a debate. If, for instance, he has just made an impassioned statement that had no connection to anything you said, you should say something like, "I'm sorry, but I seem to have missed your question. What exactly would you like me to answer?"

This will, generally, be enough to stop the tirade. If, however, it does not, then you will have to put an end to it by appealing to the audience. For example, you might say, "Sir, I can appreciate your point of view, but we are faced with a time problem, and I am certain there are other members of the audience who have questions. If it's all right with the ladies and gentlemen, I'd like to continue with the question and answer period. But, let me give you my word that if you will see me after the program, I will be happy to discuss your point of view at length." Then, with a smile and a nod to the hostile member, you would call for the next question.

Handled in this manner, you have given the audience the feeling that you are concerned about *them* while still retaining your calmness and dignity. You have emerged a winner.

... You Want Everyone to See What Is Happening On Stage ...

You can have the best, most thoughtful, most interesting presentation in the world, but it will count for nothing if it remains unseen. Consider it from the audience's point of view. How frustrating it is for you to have your attention directed to a map, chart, or diagram only to find that visual aid blocked, either wholly or partially, by the speaker's body. What makes it even worse, is that more often than not, the speaker is totally unaware of the problem.

Obviously, this is no problem when you are addressing a small, intimate group where everyone is afforded an unobstructed view of everything, or where they may move themselves or their chairs in order to obtain that view. It is when you are appearing on a stage or dais, before a larger audience, that this may prove a difficulty. Surprisingly enough, it is within the physical layout of the stage that your solution to the problem lies.

Most halls or auditoriums are set up so that the chairs for the audience are placed in rows, from just before the foot of the stage backward to the far wall of the room. The chairs on either end of these rows are usually set up in line with the proscenium arch on either side of the stage.

Therefore, if you will conceive of your shoulders as pointers, it will become obvious that your audience will always be able to see you and your display if, when you are facing to your left, you keep your right shoulder pointed at the right proscenium arch, and, when you are facing to your right, you keep your left shoulder pointed at the left proscenium arch. If you can picture this in your mind, you will see that this affords every member of the audience, in every seat, a clear line of sight to what is happening on the stage.

You will also find it useful if, when gesturing, you gesture with the hand or arm that is closest to the back wall of the stage, that is, the arm furthest away from the audience. If you will keep this in mind, you will never "reach across yourself" when gesturing, which is very unattractive from the audience's point of view, and can also block your speech and your display.

Certainly, everything you do to make your presentation as pleasant, clear, and intelligible as possible will aid in establishing rapport with your audience and leaving them in a receptive mood. You will find that the gratification your audience displays will make any effort on your part well worthwhile.

...You Are Asked a Hostile Question...

Does the term "hostile question" really need a definition? It is any question which is so stated as to put you on the spot. Please understand, we are not talking about a difficult or intricate question that is honestly asked. Rather, we mean the "When did you stop beating your wife?" variety that begs the question and whose sole intent is to put you in an unfavorable light.

You can deal effectively with a hostile question if you make certain to:

1. Remain calm and treat the questioner with respect and courtesy.
2. Break the question into its simplest parts, both stated and unstated, and answer each part separately.

Now, let's examine both steps.

First, it is essential that you remain calm. You can think more clearly and you will gain the respect of your audience if you stay rational in the face of hostility. Treating the hostile questioner with courtesy and civility will further aid in swinging the audience's support to your side.

Next, make sure that everyone knows exactly what is being asked. Let's assume that someone has asked this question: "What makes you feel so superior and that you have all the answers?" (We think you'll agree that that's a hostile question.) Here is a response that will exemplify Step Two: "I'd like to answer that question, but as I see it, you have asked several questions. I think you're really asking *if* I feel superior; *if* I do, then what makes me feel so; and *do I* have all the answers? The answers are 'no,' 'it doesn't follow,' and 'no.' Now, let's examine each one of them in turn . . .''

By handling the hostile question in this manner, you have turned a potentially embarrassing situation into one which will be advantageous to you by gaining the respect of the audience and perhaps the hostile questioner as well.

. . . Your AVA Equipment Fails . . .

The overhead projector fails to project; the bulb of the slide projector blows out halfway through the show; the film breaks, leaving you with a blank screen. These are just a few of the bothersome interruptions that can occur when your audio-visual aids fail.

No matter how you test beforehand, there is always the possibility with any mechanical device that it will break down and, if you listen to some people, at the worst possible moment. The way to deal with these interruptions is to anticipate them and be prepared for them.

If you are supplying your own equipment, make certain that an extra bulb, repair tools, and the like are part and parcel of your AVA package. If the group you are addressing is to supply the equipment, make it a condition of your appearance that they have the necessary replacement materials on hand, and check ahead of time to see that they have honored their promise.

If you are going to use a blackboard or other writing device to be seen by a group, make certain you have a back-up such as several large sheets of posterboard and a dark marker.

In other words, be prepared.

If something should happen, however, take it in a good-natured, these-things-happen manner, openly ask that it be fixed and make certain that the work is begun. In the meantime, you might fill in by discussing what was seen thus far and/or taking questions from the audience.

In any event, if you have prepared for the failure of your AVA equipment, and if, when it happens, you take it in a matter-of-fact manner, you will find that, while bothersome, these interruptions can be dealt with and overcome.

. . . You "Forget" Your Speech . . .

It is, of course, the ultimate nightmare of the public speaker. He is introduced, rises and addresses the audience, speaks a sentence or two, and then *forgets the rest of his speech*! There he is, an audience waiting patiently for his words, and he can't remember what he is to say! It is a fear which has plagued many a speaker.

Fortunately, it is a fear which is largely unfounded. It has never happened to us in years of speaking, and we know of no other speaker who has undergone that particular trauma. That is not to say, however, that it cannot or will not happen to you.

There is, of course, an old actor's trick for keying the memory. If you are in the middle of a speech and forget your next line, you clear your mind and go back and repeat the last line you said. This will, supposedly, trigger your memory. There is an easier way.

If you will look objectively at the problem, you will see that the only way you can forget a speech is if you are delivering it from memory. The solution would seem amazingly simple—don't give it from memory!

Please understand, we are not suggesting that you stand up and blandly read your speech to the audience; that would be dull and boring. There is nothing, however, which states that you cannot have that speech or a detailed outline written down, have it at the rostrum before you, and refer to it from time to time.

By all means, deliver your speech in as natural, unaffected, and spontaneous a manner as possible, but also make certain that you have your speech with you, either typed on paper or on note cards, and keep abreast of your position in the speech at all times. That way, should you go astray, you will have a handy road map to put you back on the right path.

Your audience will benefit, and so will you.

. . . Your Microphone Dies in the Middle of Your Speech . . .

This is probably *the* most common mishap faced by a speaker. You've worked and worked on your speech, practiced your gestures, and made up your displays and/or handouts. Everything is going beautifully, then right in the middle of it comes a squeal of feedback and the lonely sound of your voice—minus amplification.

This problem demands speed. You must do something quickly, or you will lose that fine rapport you have built with your audience.

Before you do anything else, check the microphone itself. Some have buttons or switches which can slip into the 'OFF' position seemingly by themselves. Make certain the switch is on. Next, *tap* the microphone head. *Do Not Blow in It.* If you hear nothing and all switches are on, it is pretty safe to assume that it is dead. Now *you* must take charge.

What you do next will depend on whether or not you can project your voice. If you can, ask your audience to indicate *by show of hands* how many of them *can* hear you. Keep it positive. Let your audience tell you what they *can do,* not what they can't. If you cannot project, raise your voice as much as you can *without* shouting, and then ask the question. The tonal quality of your voice must be comfortable for both you and your audience. In either case, when you ask your audience if they can hear you, do so in a tone of voice in which you would be capable of continuing. If more than 80% of your audience raises their hands, you may proceed to the next step.

Leave the podium. Bring your notes with you, but get out from behind the lectern. You must give every indication to your audience that you are thinking of their well-being, not your own momentary inconvenience. Come as close to the edge of the stage or dais as you possibly can. Even if you must step out of a spotlight, it is better that your audience hear you clearly, than see you. As soon as you have the audience back with you, you will proceed to choose one of several options.

You must start "reading" your audience at this point. As long as they are comfortable, you will continue. If they become agitated, squirmy, or inattentive, be ready to change. If you are near the end of your speech (no more than one page away), go ahead and finish. If, however, you still have a great deal of material to cover, interrupt yourself. Tell your audience that you realize that they are not comfortable and that you are certain the microphone will be fixed shortly. Because you have polled them before continuing, you are sure that your decision will be met favorably. Moreover, the interruption at this point does not break the rapport, but it actually strengthens it.

Following these steps will aid you in overcoming this annoying problem. It will go even quicker if you have taken that "ounce of prevention" by asking the person in charge of the microphone where you are speaking what procedures he intends to follow should it fail. This precludes the spare microphone being located five blocks away in some dusty storeroom.

... You Are Faced with a Tired and/or Restless Audience ...

While these two audiences are not entirely alike, the problems they pose to the speaker and the speaker's solutions to those problems are somewhat similar. First, let's define terms: the tired audience has usually been sitting or has been involved with a program for some length of time. They have been called upon by others to give their attention to a particular matter, and now you are going to do the same thing. Everything about them is telling you that they've had enough concentrating. The restless audience, on the other hand, usually has an axe to grind. They want to get out of there, but you have to speak first; they've just come back (from lunch or a break) and haven't settled into the program; they want to hear a particular speaker who is coming up just after your speech; the last event or speaker has excited them.

The solution to handling the tired audience may seem strange at first, but we have seen it work, and we have used it effectively ourselves. It involves two steps:

1. Acknowledge that they are tired.
2. Call for a stretch break.

Say, "It's been a long day (meeting, afternoon, evening, etc.)." Wait for a moment and there will surely be a few giggles and laughs. "I think," you continue, "that if I had to sit for another minute I'd have developed unmentionable calluses. I would not want the same fate to befall you, so why don't we all stand up for a moment. That's right, stand up. Stretch your arms out like this. That's right. Shake hands with your neighbor. Say, 'Hi, Neighbor.' That's it!''

These are the words that we would use, but you must suit what you say to your own personality. In any event, we have found that this brief respite is welcomed by the audience. It causes a laugh or two, completely dissolves tension, and puts the audience into a much more receptive state of mind when you do begin to speak than they would have had had you ignored the fact.

The *restless* audience cannot be handled across-the-board. Here, you must pinpoint the reason for their restlessness, deal with it, and get their attention back to you as the speaker. Here, you will have to use your own judgment. If a previous speaker or program has excited them, then remark, ''Wasn't that a fantastic speech that Mr. Jones just gave. I think he deserves another round of applause.'' Then lead the applause yourself. Let the audience get it out of their system before *you* begin. If they are anxious to get out, and you are the last speaker, then acknowledge that fact, give every indication that you will hurry (but never hurry your speech), and tell them how important what you have to say will be. It would come out something like this, (again, use *your* words, not ours) ''I have some good news, and some bad news. First the good news—I am the last speaker. Now the bad news—I have to speak before you can go home. Actually, I hope you won't find it a very traumatic experience, since I have something to say which, I feel, has tremendous bearing on what has been said this evening . . .'' If your audience is still coming back from lunch and are finding seats, talking, etc., then stop what you are doing and wait, that's right, wait, until they are quiet. Remember the old teaching tactic—never talk to a moving mass! They will quiet down quickly, and you can continue.

The tired and/or restless audience faces the speaker with a challenge which, with good humor, good naturedness, and the speaker's knowledge of what he will do and say in the situation, can be effectively overcome.

. . . You Are Nervous . . .

Actors call it "stage fright"; radio announcers call it "mike fright"; and you may call it what you will, but it is that feeling, just before you are introduced, that your knees have turned to water, your spine is made of jelly, your voice has just departed for parts unknown, and you would rather be anywhere—from an arctic iceberg to the middle of a desert sandstorm—than where you are. It is something that happens and something with which you must deal. If it is any comfort to you, Helen Hayes, that marvelous veteran actress of thousands and thousands of public appearances, once reported that before every public appearance she ever made, she got so nervous as to become physically ill. Yet anyone who has ever had the honor of watching her perform will know that never once was that anxiety communicated to her audiences.

What is the solution to this problem? Many have been proffered. We were once told to picture the audience sitting there in their underwear. The picture becomes so ludicrous that you can't possibly be nervous. Another speaker told us that he never looks at the audience, but focuses on the hairline of audience members. This gives the impression of looking directly at them without having eye contact.

Each of these solutions worked for the person who used them. We have never had to. Yes, we have been nervous, but here, a matter of philosophy has always been our salvation. We have always expected to love every audience to whom we spoke, and we have expected them to love us. We have not been disappointed. Nervous, certainly, but the minute the first words come forth, we get interested in *them*—the audience—and we forget *our*selves, *our* problems, and most importantly of all, *our* nervousness.

Try it; it works.

Index